CW01584208

STANDARD GRADE

GEOGRAPHY

QUESTIONS AND SKILLS

JOHN GREENLEES

Hodder & Stoughton

A MEMBER OF THE HODDER HEADLINE GROUP

ACKNOWLEDGEMENTS

The publishers would like to thank the following for permission to reproduce materials in this book. Every effort has been made to trace and acknowledge all copyright holders, but if any have been overlooked, the publishers will be pleased to make the necessary arrangements.

Ordnance Survey mapping, with the permission of The Controller of Her Majesty's Stationery Office © Crown copyright, Map 1

All photographs belong to the author.

All inside artwork by 1–11 Line Art.

Cataloguing in Publication Data is available from the British Library

ISBN 0 340 69121 2

First published 1997
Impression number 10 9 8 7 6 5 4 3 2 1
Year 2000 1999 1998 1997

Typeset by Wearset, Boldon, Tyne and Wear.
Printed in Great Britain for Hodder & Stoughton Educational, a division of Hodder Headline Plc, 338 Euston Road, London NW1 3BH by The Bath Press, Bath.

Contents

INTRODUCTION

Standard Grade Geography: Questions and Skills provides around 100 exam-style questions, and a similar number of information sources, to help develop knowledge and understanding of the 17 Key Ideas and seven Concepts which make up the Standard Grade Geography course.

The questions also provide invaluable practice at analysing and interpreting the maps, diagrams, graphs, tables of statistics, newspaper extracts and other information sources which are used in exam questions. A section on Information Handling Skills has been included to provide notes and advice on how to extract information from these sources and how to evaluate the information which is extracted. There are also questions to help develop important investigative and enquiry skills including collecting, analysing and presenting information. A detailed glossary has been included at the back of the book to explain the meaning of key words.

The questions have been differentiated, with relatively easy ones at the beginning of each chapter and then progressively more difficult ones to challenge faster learners. The **Core questions** are Foundation and General Level questions, while the **Extension tasks** are General and Credit Level questions.

THE 17 KEY IDEAS

The Physical Environment

1 Physical landscapes are the product of natural processes and are always changing.
2 The elements of weather can be identified, observed, measured, recorded and classified. As a result, dynamic patterns can be identified and used for forecasting.
3 The world can be divided into major climatic zones.
4 The physical environment offers a range of possibilities for, and limitations on, human activities.
5 There are many competing demands for the use of rural landscapes.
6 The physical environment is a resource which has to be used with care and its management is a global issue.

The Human Environment

7 Settlements have many common characteristics relating to site, situation and function.
8 Urban settlements have dynamic patterns relating to their size, form and function.
9 Farming systems provide food supplies and raw materials.
10 The viability of manufacturing industry is affected by a variety of factors.
11 Economic change has social and environmental consequences.

International Issues

12 Population is unevenly distributed.
13 Populations have measurable social and economic characteristics.
14 In any area, the size and structure of the population are subject to change.
15 International relations are dominated by a limited number of countries acting in conjunction with others.
16 Regions of the world are linked through trade.
17 Schemes of self help, along with national and international aid, seek to encourage social and economic development.

THE SEVEN CONCEPTS

- **change** – how physical and human systems change through time
- **conflict** – the disagreements which arise over local and national issues
- **co-operation** – how local, national and international problems can be overcome by people working together
- **diversity** – the variety of environmental, social and economic activities
- **inter-dependence** – how different places and different groups of people rely on each other
- **location** – where different places can be found
- **spatial patterns** – the spread or pattern of places.

There are a number of different types of information sources which are used in Standard Grade Geography. It is important that you can recognise and understand how to use these different sources and are able to extract as much information as possible from them. The types of information sources used in Standard Grade Geography are as follows:

- maps including Ordnance Survey extracts, weather charts and cartograms
- graphs including bar graphs, line graphs, pie charts, dissected bar diagrams and scatter graphs
- diagrams including flow diagrams, cross-sections and transects
- photographs and sketches
- newspaper extracts
- cartoons.

MAPS

Three of the different types of maps used in Standard Grade Geography are shown as Maps 1, 2 and 3.

Map 1 (on the inside back cover) is a 1:50 000 **Ordnance Survey 'Landranger' map.**

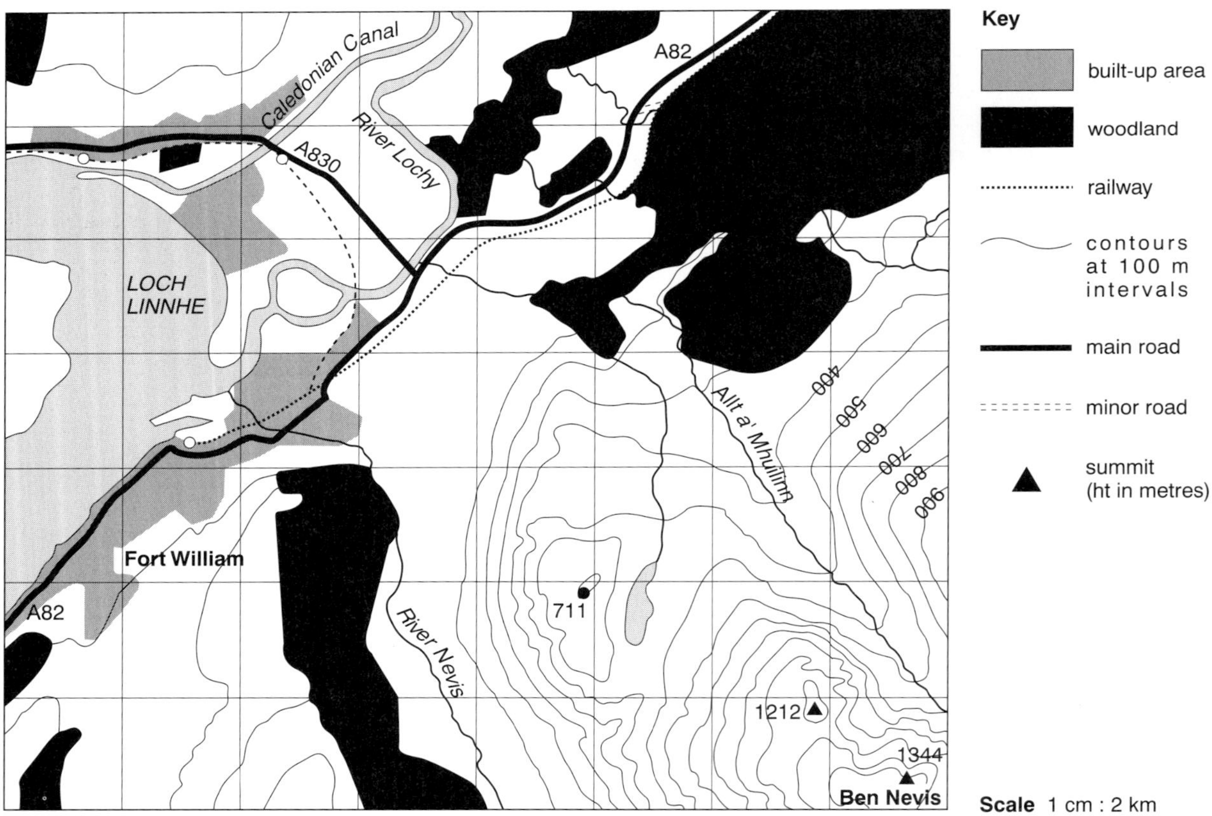

MAP 2 A relief map of the Fort William area

For OS maps, you should know how to read and give grid references and be able to identify the different map symbols. Remember that four-figure grid references are used to identify entire grid squares, while six-figure grid references are used to identify exact points on maps. On Map 1 bonded warehouses can be found in grid square 8394 while the red dot which represents Stirling railway station can be found at 798936.

Map 2 (on page 6) is a **relief map** which uses contour lines to show the shape and height of the land. Remember that contour lines close together indicate steep slopes, while contour lines which are far apart indicate flat or gently-sloping land.

Map 3 is a **cartogram** (or map-diagram) which highlights a particular feature – in this case the populations of the main regions of the world.

Here are some tips on how to extract information from maps:

- look at the title of the map to find out more about what the map shows
- look at the key of the map to see what the different shades and symbols mean
- use the scale of the map to work out the real distance between places
- with relief maps (including Ordnance Survey maps), use contour lines to work out heights and to determine the shape of the land.

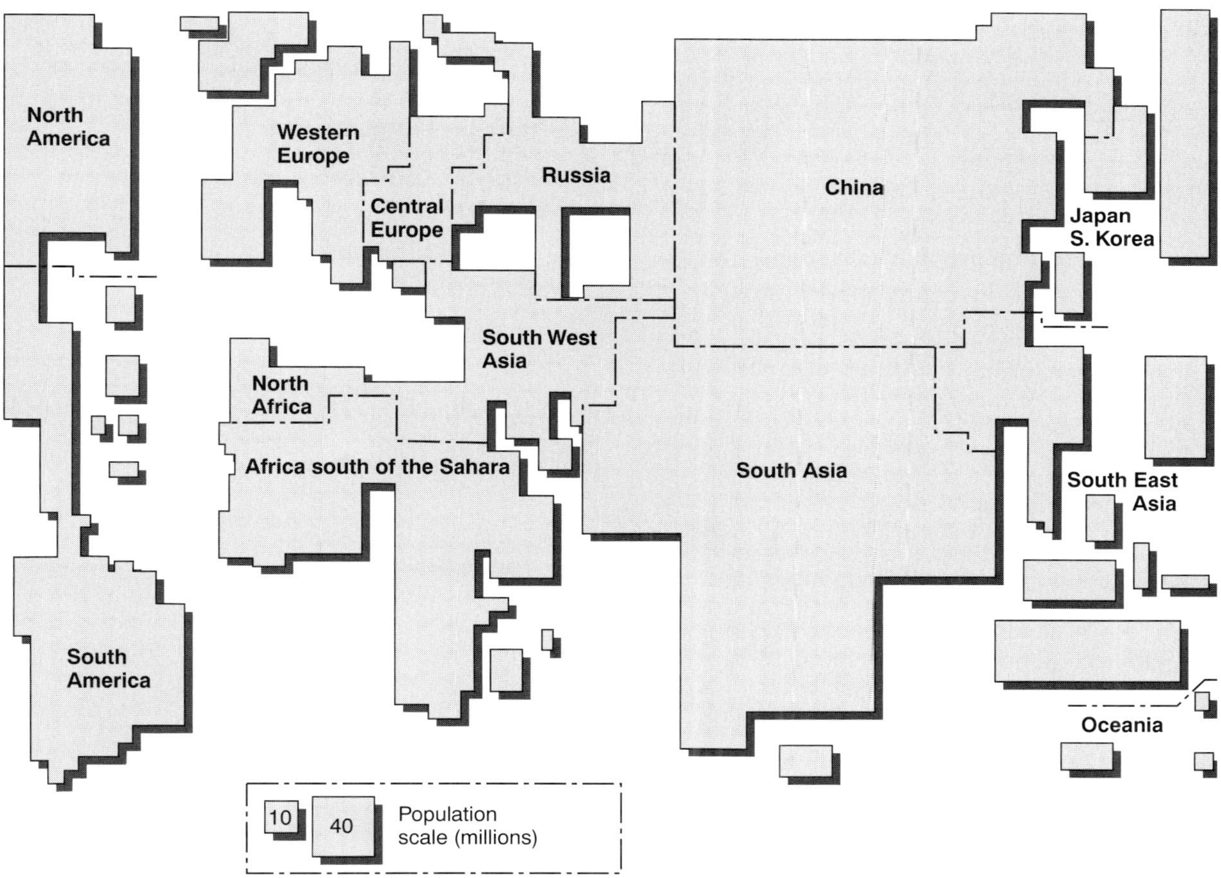

MAP 3 A cartogram showing the regions of the world in proportion to the sizes of their populations

GRAPHS

Some of the different types of graphs used in Standard Grade Geography are shown as Graphs 1 to 6.

Graph 1 is a **bar graph** which uses bars to show comparisons – in this case a comparison of the life expectancy figures of six countries.

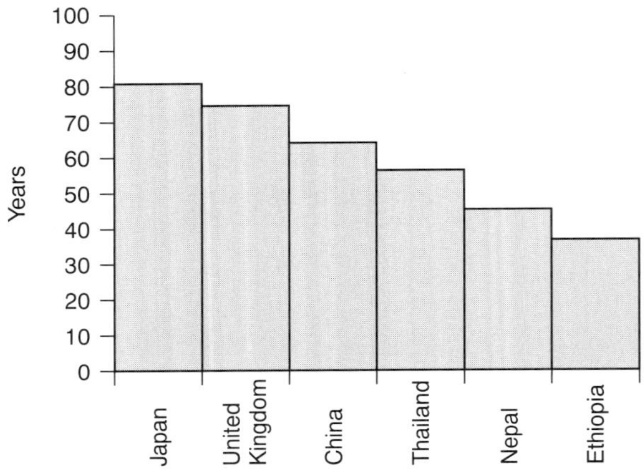

GRAPH 1 A bar graph showing life expectancy

Graph 2 is a **line graph** which uses a line to show how something changes over time – in this case the price of oil.

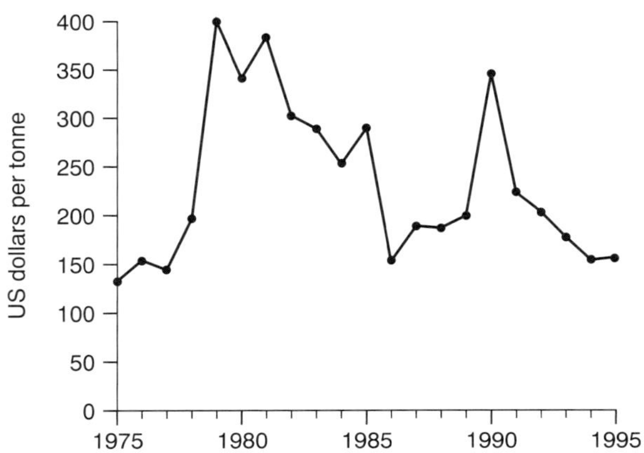

GRAPH 2 A line graph showing the price of oil

Graph 3 is a **pie chart** which shows the relative importance of different elements – in this case Scotland's main land uses.

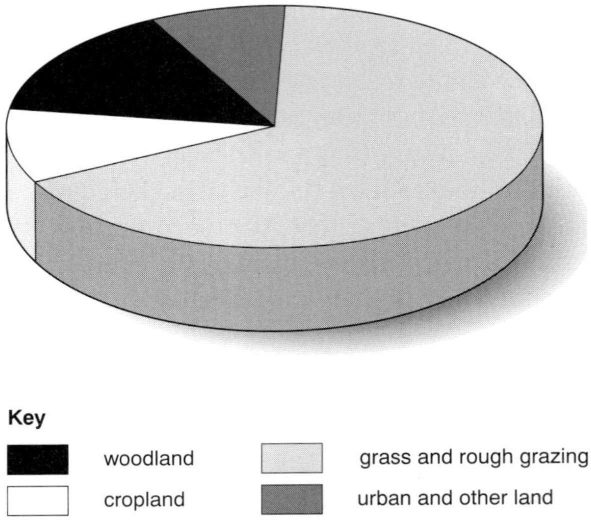

GRAPH 3 A pie chart showing land use in Scotland

Graph 4 is a **dissected bar diagram** which also shows the relative importance of different elements – in this case the rural and urban populations of Scotland.

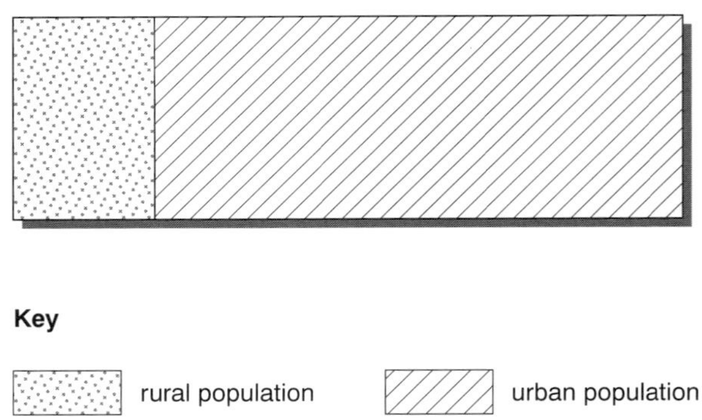

GRAPH 4 A dissected bar diagram showing the rural and urban populations of Scotland (1996)

Graph 5 is a **compound graph** which uses bars and lines to show information about the climate of Edinburgh.

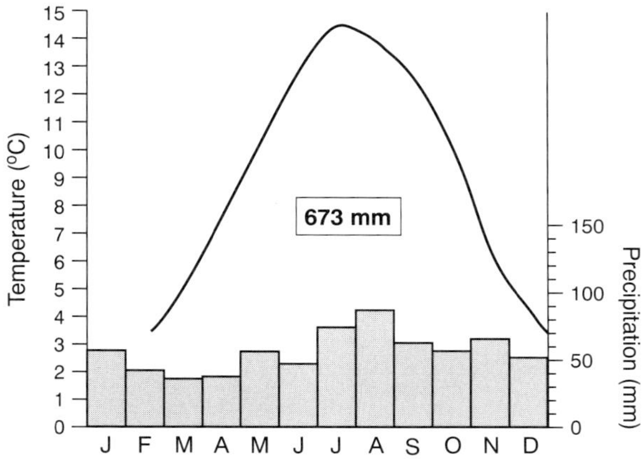

GRAPH 5 A compound graph showing the climate of Edinburgh

Graph 6 is a **scatter graph** which shows the relationship between literacy and GNP.

Here are some tips for extracting information from graphs:

- always read the title of the graph to find out more about what the graph shows
- read the information along the sides of the graph to identify the units of measurement involved – remember to use these units of measurement if you include any figures from the graph in your answer
- the total area of pie charts or dissected bar diagrams equals 100 per cent – so half the area therefore equals 50 per cent, a quarter equals 25 per cent and a tenth equals 10 per cent
- try and identify the changes, patterns or trends shown by the graph.

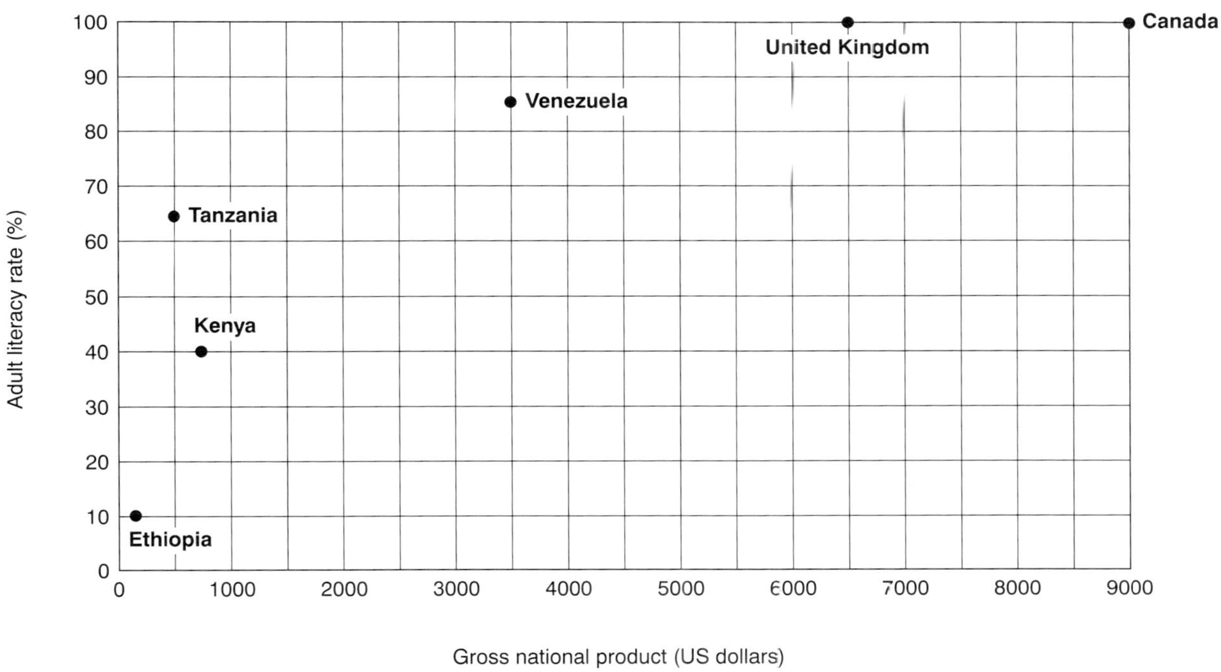

GRAPH 6 A scatter graph showing the relationship between literacy and GNP

DIAGRAMS

The diagrams used in Standard Geography include flow diagrams, cross-sections and transects.

DIAGRAM 1 A flow diagram showing the effects of the closure of a factory

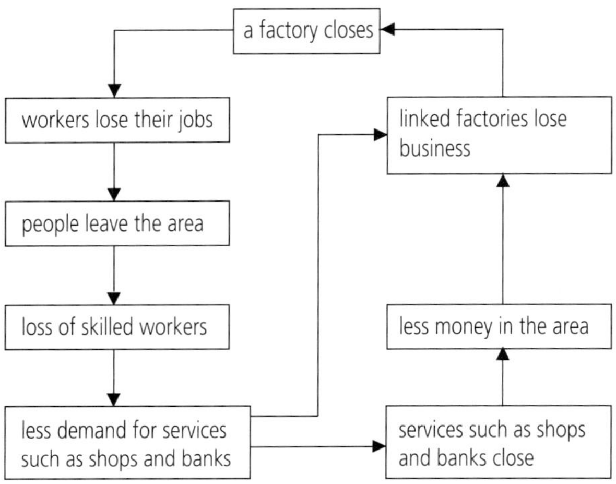

A **flow diagram** (such as Diagram 1) uses boxes and arrows to show connections and movements.

A **cross-section** (such as Diagram 2) provides a side-ways view of an area of land to enable the shape and height of the land to be studied.

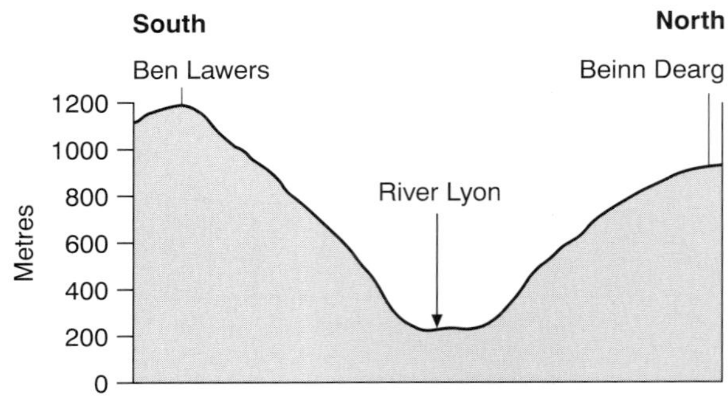

DIAGRAM 2 A cross-section of Glen Lyon

A **transect** (such as Diagram 3) is a cross-section with additional information about soils, vegetation and land use.

DIAGRAM 3 A transect of the Strathmore area

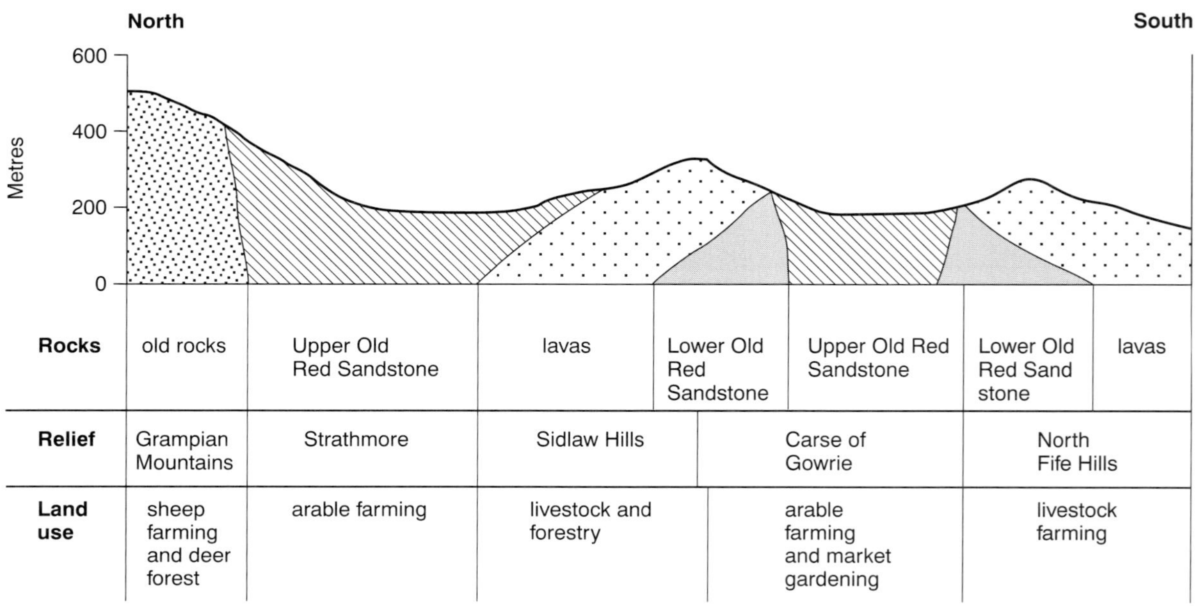

OTHER SOURCES OF INFORMATION

Other sources of information in Standard Grade Geography include sketches, photographs, newspaper extracts and cartoons. With sketches and photographs it is important to think carefully about what is being shown – there may be labels or annotations to help you with this. With photographs (such as Photograph 1) ask questions such as:

- what does the photograph show? (A settlement next to the sea.)
- what are the dominant features? (The harbour, some houses and fishing equipment.)
- what can be suggested from these features? (The settlement – St Abbs – is a small fishing village; the settlement is built on a difficult site – there isn't much flat land and houses have been built on the steeper and higher ground which lies above the harbour.)

In the case of newspaper extracts, it is important to recognise key words or facts. For cartoons, look for bias or exaggeration. Bias is when a distorted or prejudiced view is given, while exaggeration is when something is made to sound much better or much worse than it actually is.

PHOTOGRAPH 1 St Abbs

ANSWERING EXAM QUESTIONS

Finally, here are some tips for answering Standard Grade exam questions:

- look for the key words and instructions in a question; some of the most important key words are listed below.
- look at the number of marks for each question – questions with more marks require longer and more detailed answers
- leave spaces at the end of each answer so that you can write in any additional points you may remember later

Key Words in Exam Questions

- **compare** – outline the similarities and differences
- **describe** – outline the main features or characteristics
- **explain** – give reasons
- **identify** – point out and name
- **outline** – describe the main features or characteristics
- **rank** – put in order of size
- **state** – name or give
- **suggest** – put forward ideas or give an opinion.

1 Glaciated Landscapes and Rivers

Key Idea **Physical landscapes are the product of natural processes and are always changing.**

CORE QUESTIONS

1 (a) Look at Figure 1.1 which shows an area of land before and after glaciation. Describe the shape of:

i. the hills before glaciation
ii. the hills after glaciation
iii. the valley before glaciation
iv. the valley after glaciation. (4)

FIGURE 1.1 An area of land before and after glaciation

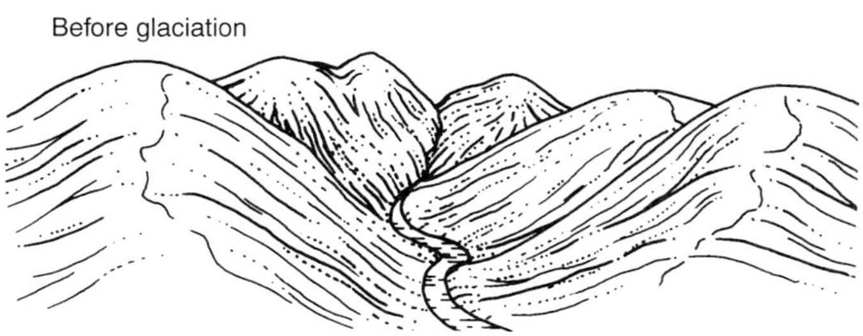

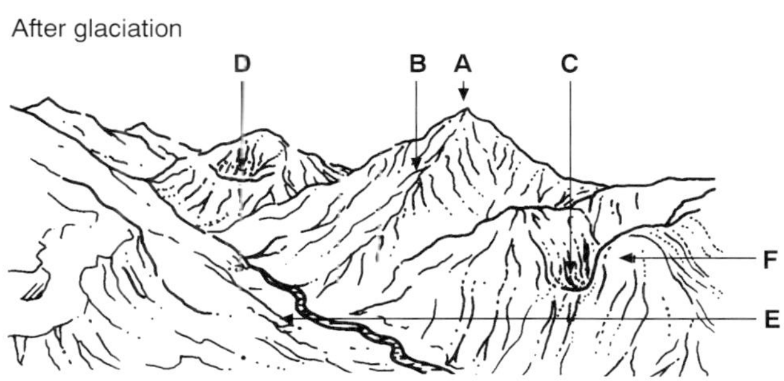

(b) Identify the landforms labelled **A** to **F** in Figure 1.1. Choose from:

corrie
hanging valley
pyramidal peak
U-shaped valley
truncated spur
arête (6)

(c) Glaciers are still shaping the land in some of the higher parts of Europe. Name two countries in Europe where (2)

(12)

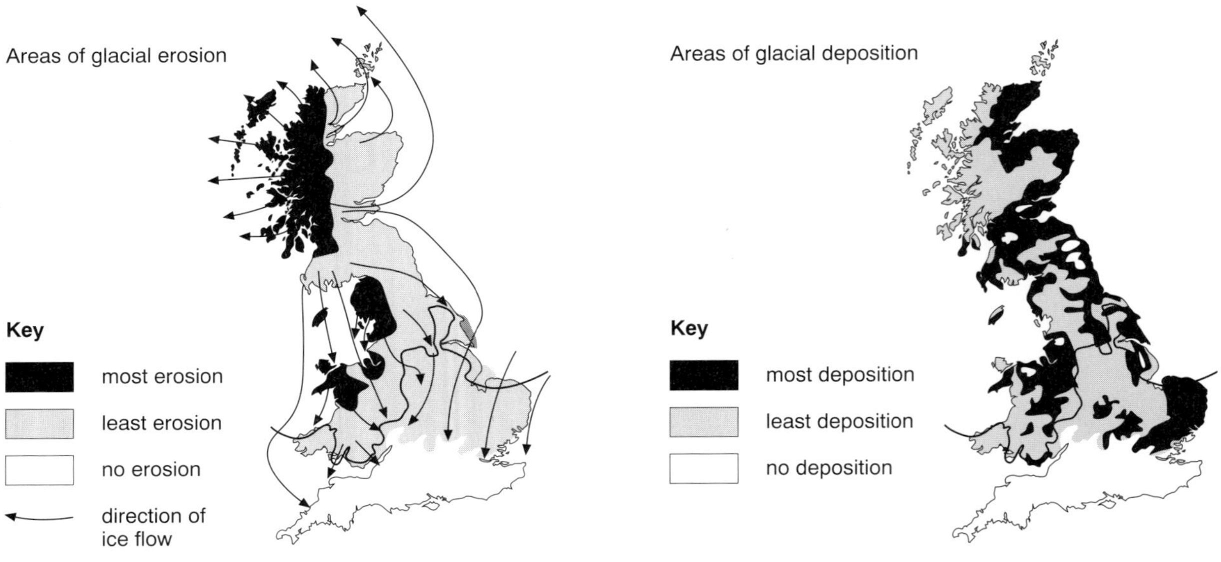

FIGURE 1.2 Areas of glacial erosion and deposition in Scotland, England and Wales

2 Figure 1.2 shows areas of glacial erosion and deposition in Scotland, England and Wales.

(a) Name:

i. two areas affected by glacial erosion
ii. two areas affected by glacial deposition. (4)

(b) Why is the very southern part of England neither an area of glacial erosion nor an area of glacial deposition? (2)

(6)

3 Study Figure 1.3 which shows the valley of the River Devon in central Scotland.

(a) List three differences between the upper course of the River Devon and the lower course of the River Devon. (3)

(b) Name the river features shown at:

i. **A**
ii. **B**
iii. **C**. (3)

(6)

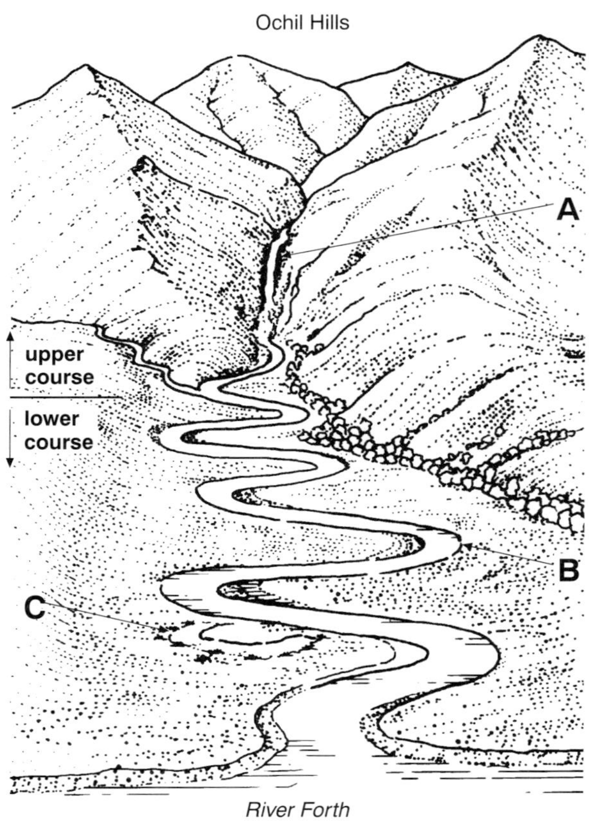

FIGURE 1.3 The valley of the River Devon

EXTENSION TASKS

4 Look at Figure 1.4 which shows the formation of a corrie.
Copy the sketch and then add labels to explain what is happening. (6)

(6)

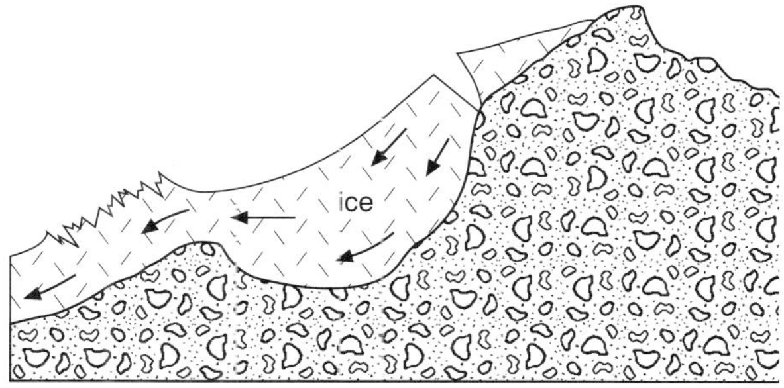

FIGURE 1.4 The formation of a corrie

5 Study Figure 1.5 which shows a landscape during and after glaciation.

(a) In which direction did the ice retreat? Give a reason for your answer. (2)

(b) What landscape features have been formed by glacial deposition? Name and describe four different features. (4)

(6)

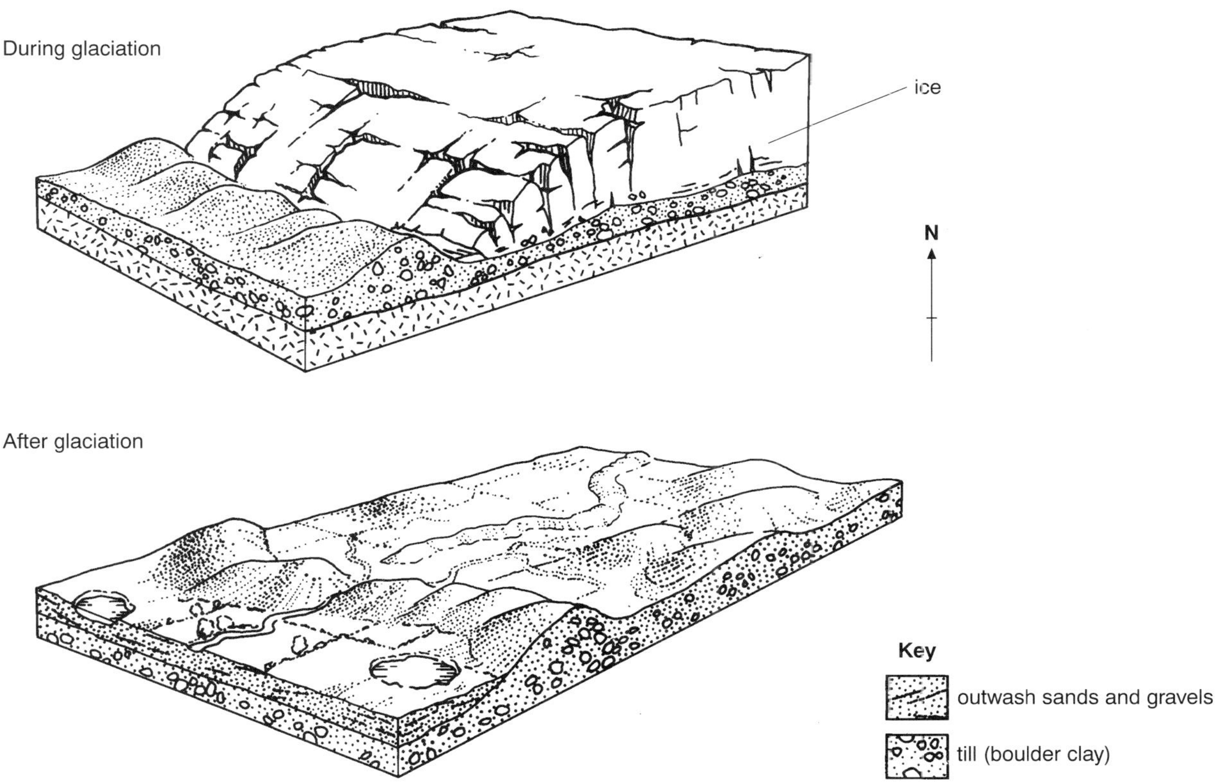

FIGURE 1.5 An area of land during and after glaciation

6 Look at Figure 1.6 which shows three cross-section views of river valleys.

(a) Describe the different shapes of the valleys noting whether they would be found in the upper, middle or lower course of a river. (3)

(b) Explain why different parts of river valleys have different shapes. (3)

(c) Study the Ordnance Survey map on the inside back cover. Describe the river course and physical features of the River Forth between GR 770962 and GR 840936. (3)

(d) For any one of the physical features you mentioned in your answer to **(c)**, draw a sketch to describe how the feature was formed. (3)

(12)

TOTAL NUMBER OF MARKS **48**

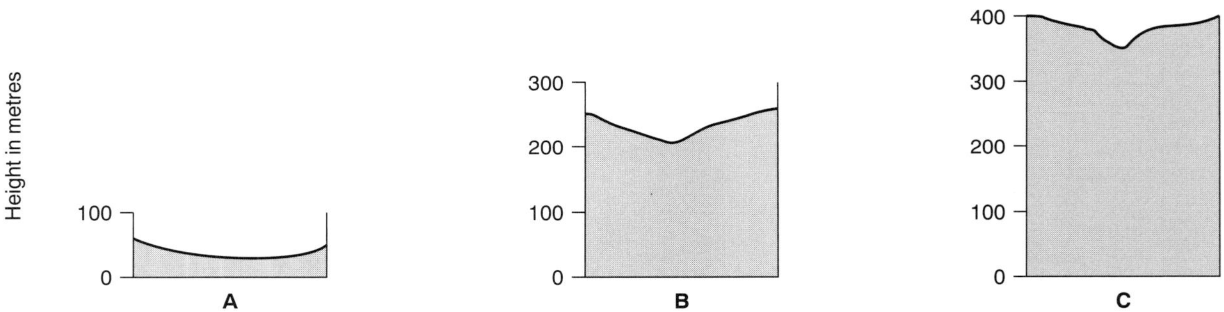

FIGURE 1.6 Three cross-section views of river valleys

2 Weather

Key Idea **The elements of the weather can be identified, observed, measured, recorded and classified. As a result, dynamic patterns can be identified and used for forecasting.**

CORE QUESTIONS

1 Look at Figure 2.1 which shows a weather station.

(a) Which instrument (**A**, **B**, **C** or **D**) is used to measure:
  i. rainfall
  ii. wind speed
  iii. hours of sunshine
  iv. wind direction? (4)

(b) Name two groups of people who are interested in information about:
  i. wind direction
  ii. hours of sunshine
  iii. rainfall. (6)

(c) Name two elements of the weather which are not measured by instruments. (2)

(12)

FIGURE 2.1 A weather station

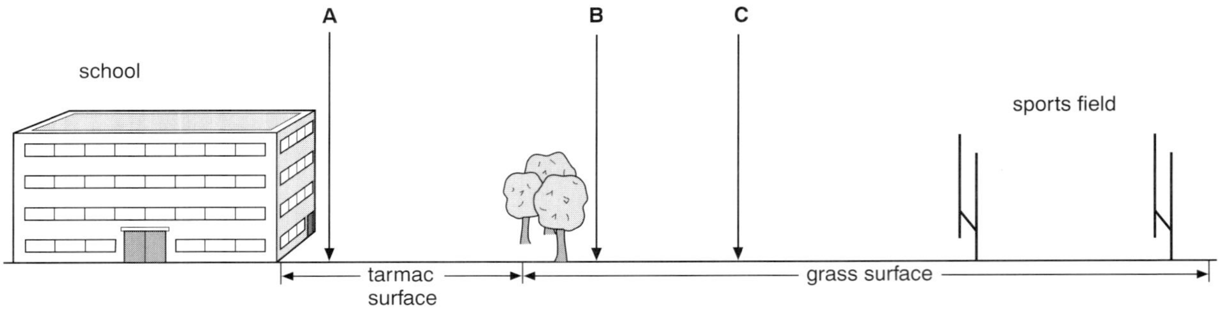

FIGURE 2.2 Possible sites for a school weather station

2 Figure 2.2 shows three possible sites for a school weather station.

(a) Which site (**A**, **B** or **C**) is the best site for a weather station?
Give two reasons for your answer. (3)

(b) What makes the other two sites unsuitable? (3)

(6)

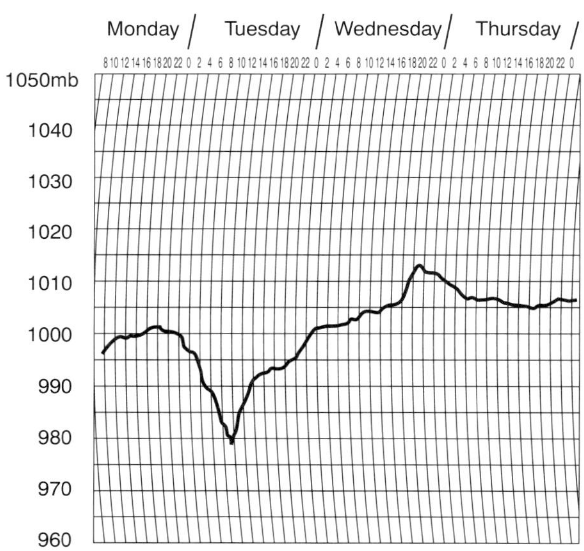

FIGURE 2.3 Changes in air pressure

3 Look at Figure 2.3 which shows changes in air pressure.

(a) Answer the following questions:
i. When was air pressure highest?
ii. When was air pressure lowest?
iii. When was a figure of 985 mb recorded?
iv. What is the name of the instrument which measures air pressure? (4)

(b) i. What is the name given to a low pressure system?
ii. Describe the type of weather which accompanies low pressure systems. (4)

(c) i. What is the name given to a high pressure system?
ii. Describe the type of weather which accompanies high pressure systems. (4)

(12)

4 Study the weather map shown as Figure 2.4.

(a) Name:

i. the type of front at **A**
ii. the type of front at **B**
iii. the type of front at **C**
iv. the sector at **D**
v. the type of line at **E**
vi. the element of the weather represented by the line at **E**. (6)

(b) i. Describe the weather conditions being experienced in Edinburgh. (3)

ii. Explain why Edinburgh is experiencing these weather conditions. (3)

(12)

FIGURE 2.4 A weather map (for 1200 hours, 15 August)

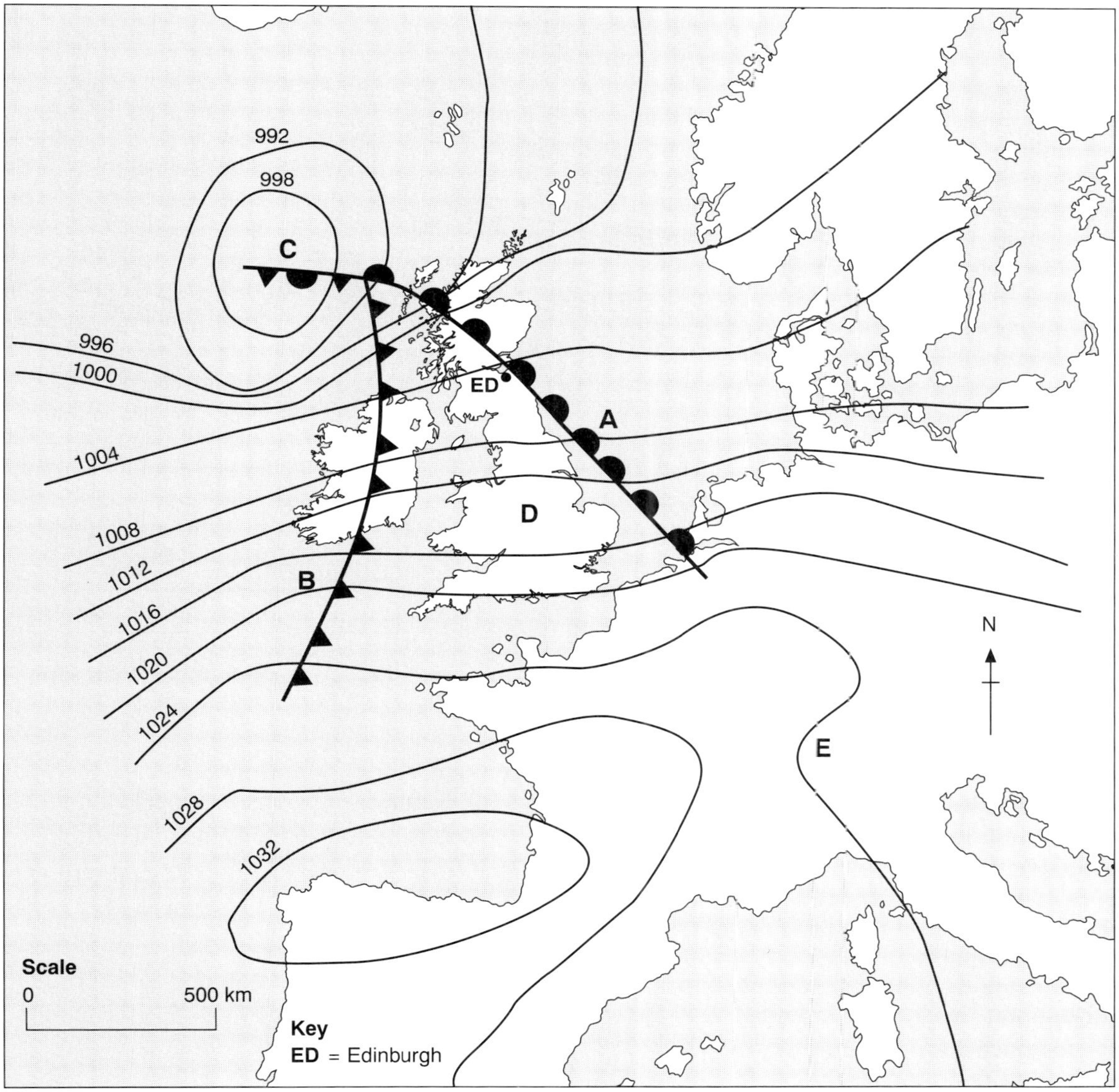

EXTENSION TASKS

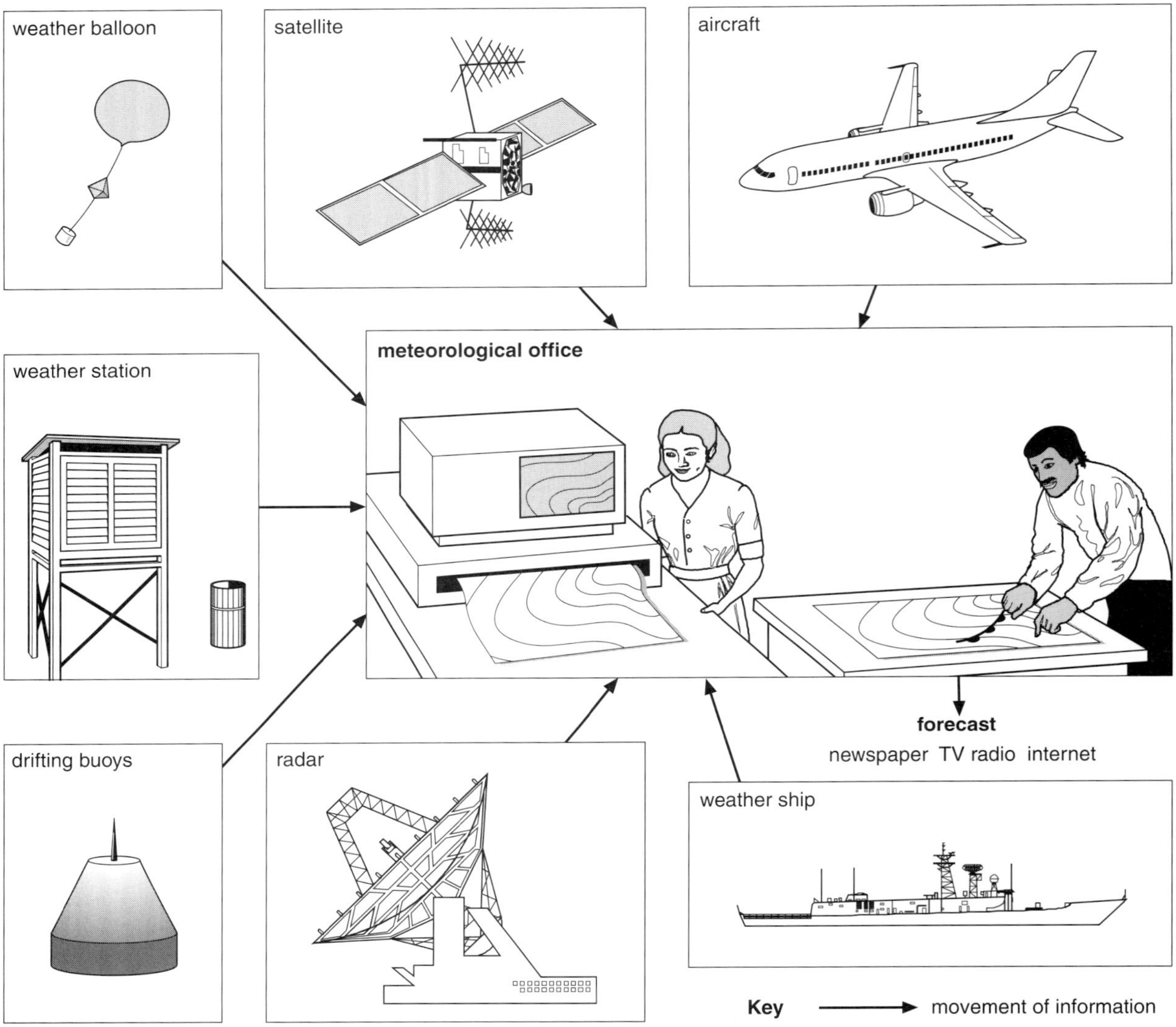

FIGURE 2.5 How information is gathered for weather forecasts

5 Look at Figure 2.5 which shows how information is gathered for weather forecasts.

(a) Describe how a weather forecast is prepared. (4)

(b) Explain how new technology has improved the accuracy of weather forecasts. (4)

(c) Name two groups of people who are willing to pay for detailed weather forecasts and outline the different ways they can obtain these forecasts. (4)

(12)

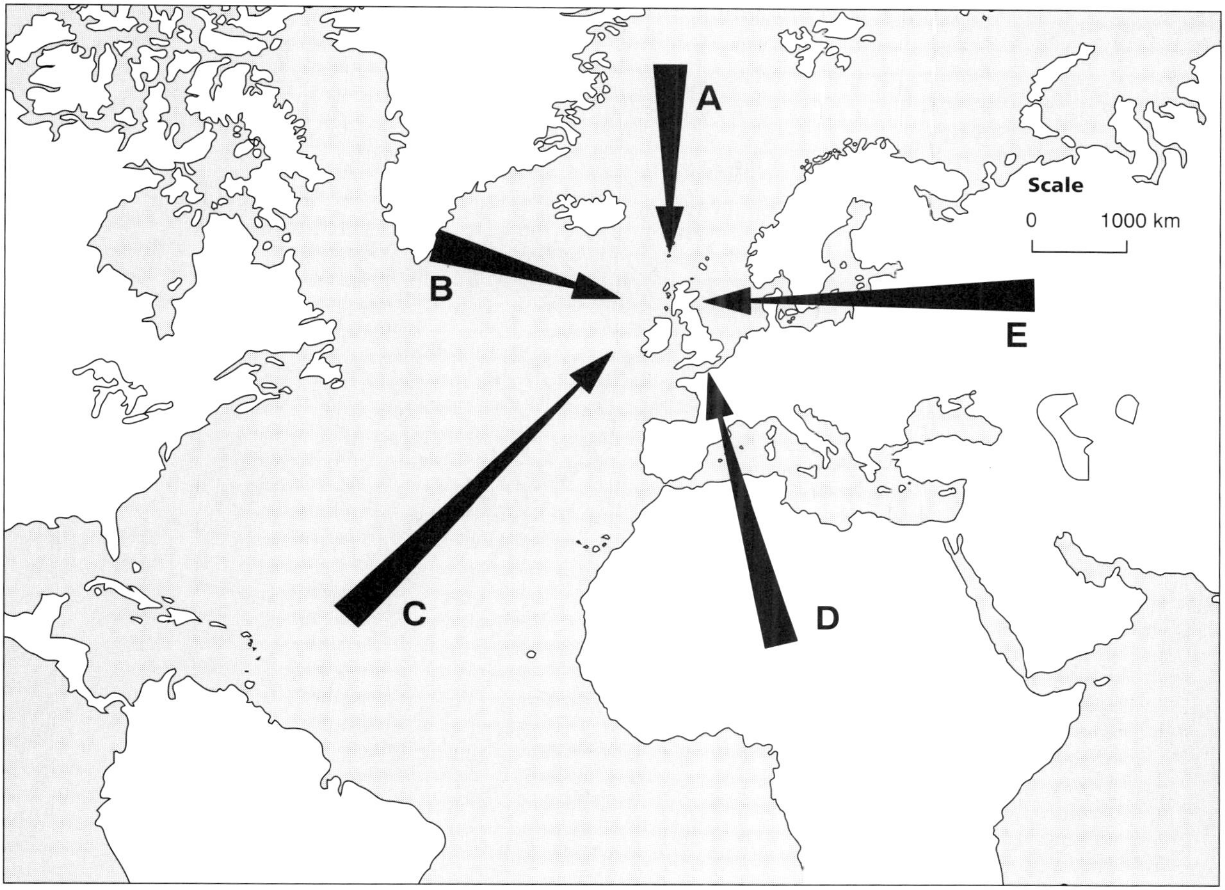

FIGURE 2.6 The air masses which affect the British Isles

6 Study Figure 2.6 which shows the air masses which affect the weather of the British Isles.

(a) Name any four of the air masses labelled **A**, **B**, **C**, **D** and **E**. (4)

(b) Describe the weather conditions which would result when:

i. air mass **A** occurs in winter

ii. air mass **D** occurs in summer. (4)

(c) Explain the different weather conditions brought by air masses **B** and **E**. (4)

(12)

7 Figure 2.7A (page 22) shows a synoptic chart while Figure 2.7B shows two weather station circles.

(a) Which of the weather station circles (**A** or **B**) shows the weather being experienced in Inverness? Explain your choice. (3)

(b) Draw a weather station circle to show the weather conditions which are likely in Paris. (3)

(6)

TOTAL NUMBER OF MARKS **72**

FIGURE 2.7A A synoptic chart (for 1200 on 20 January)

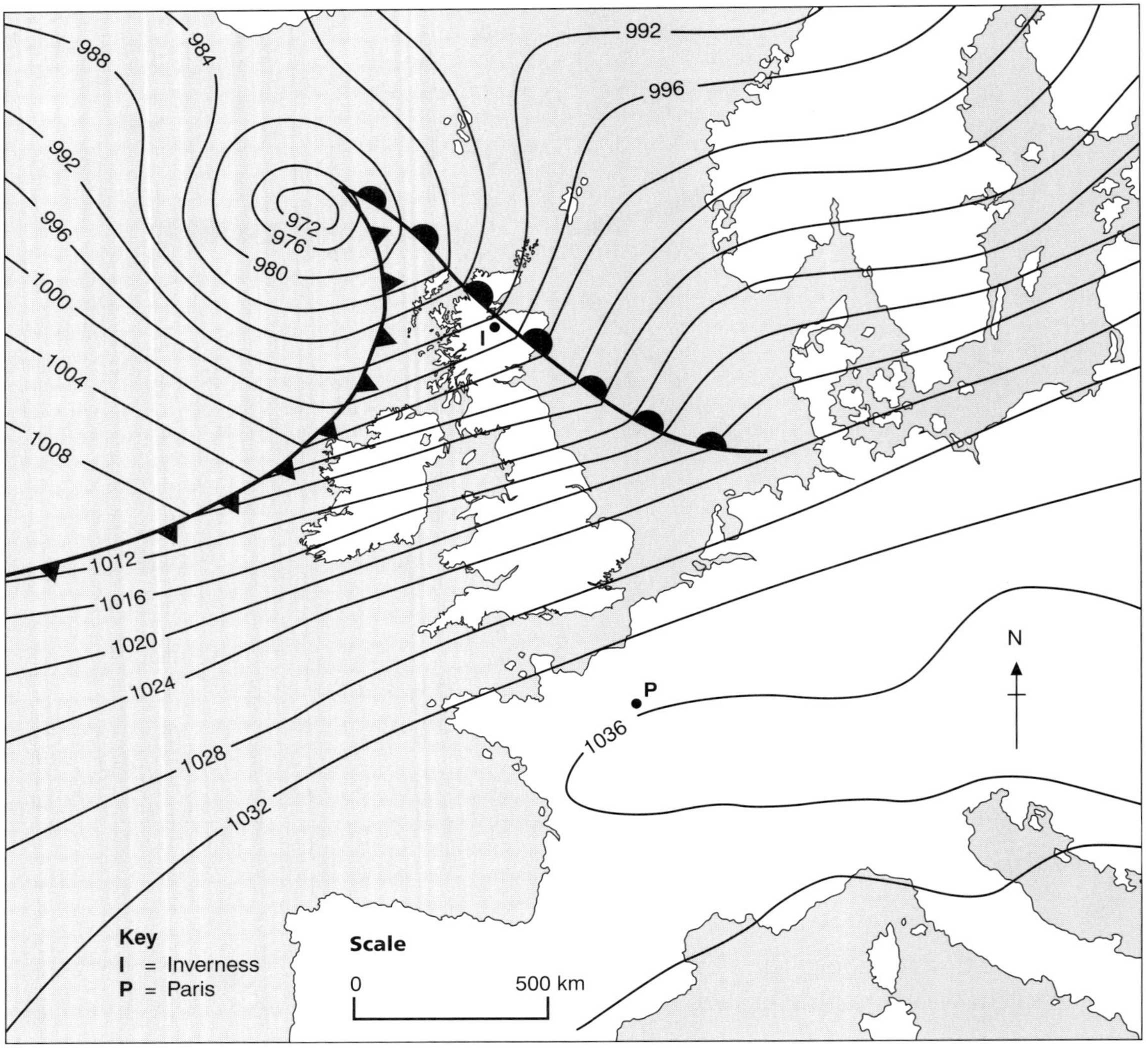

FIGURE 2.7B Two weather station circles

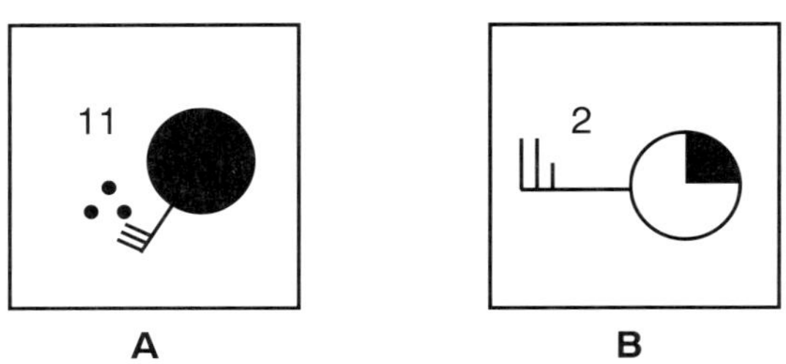

3 Climatic Regions

Key Idea **The world can be divided into major climatic zones.**

CORE QUESTIONS

1 Study 3.1 which shows four climatic regions.

(a) State which climatic region is:

i. next to the Equator

ii. next to the Tropics on the west sides of the continents

iii. in high latitudes in northern North America and northern Asia

iv. named after a sea in southern Europe. (2)

(b) State which climatic region is:

i. hot and wet all year round

ii. very cold and dry all year round

iii. hot and dry in summer and mild and wet in winter

iv. hot and dry all year round. (4)

(6)

FIGURE 3.1 Four climatic regions

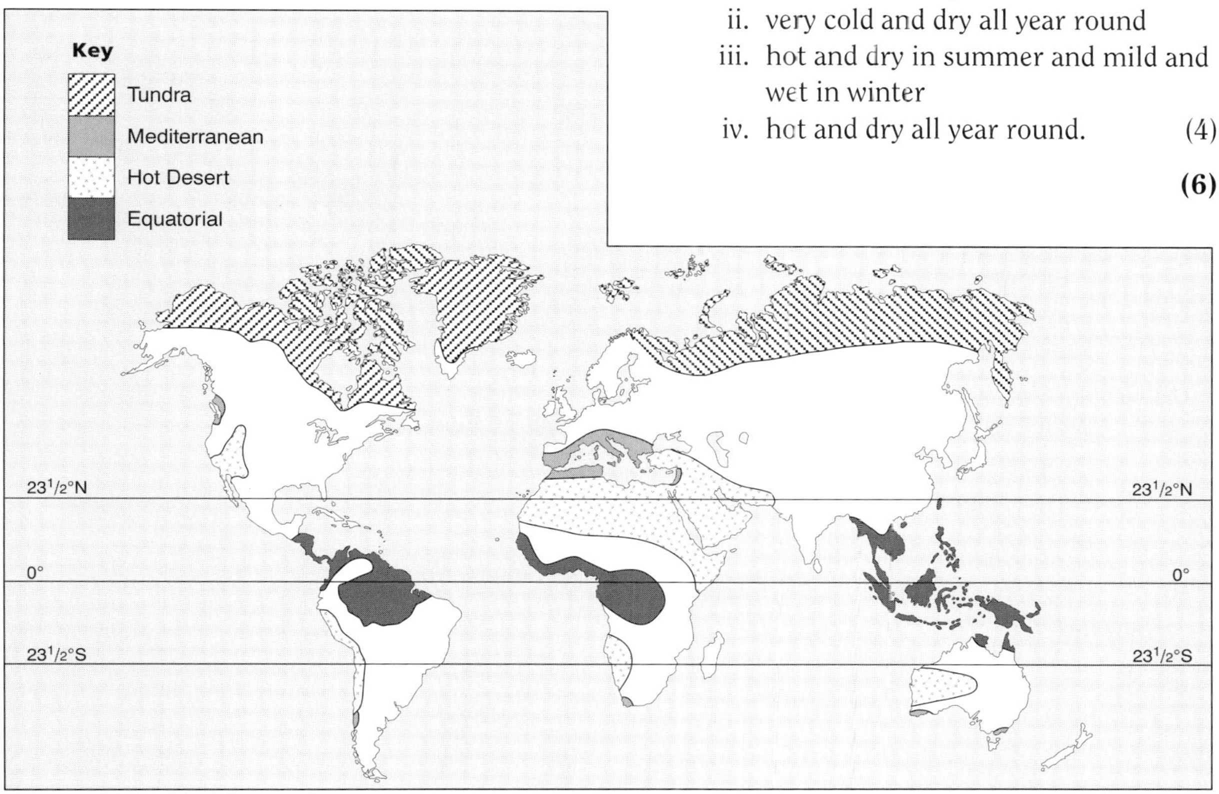

2 Look at Figure 3.2 which shows a climatic graph.

(a) What climatic region does this graph represent? (1)

(b) Describe the main features of this climatic region. (2)

(c) What makes this climatic region a difficult place in which to live and work? List two different difficulties. (3)

(6)

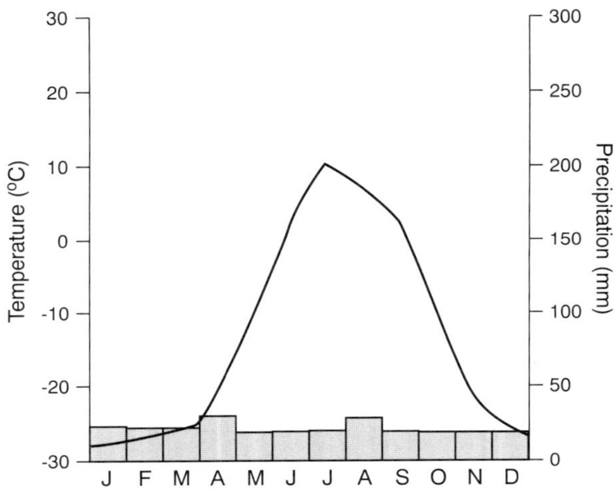

FIGURE 3.2 A climatic graph

3 Study the two climatic graphs in Figure 3.3.

(a) Answer the following questions:

i. Which graph has the biggest range of temperature?

ii. Which graph has the highest annual rainfall? (2)

(b) State two ways in which the climates are similar. (2)

(c) State two ways in which the climates are different. (2)

(6)

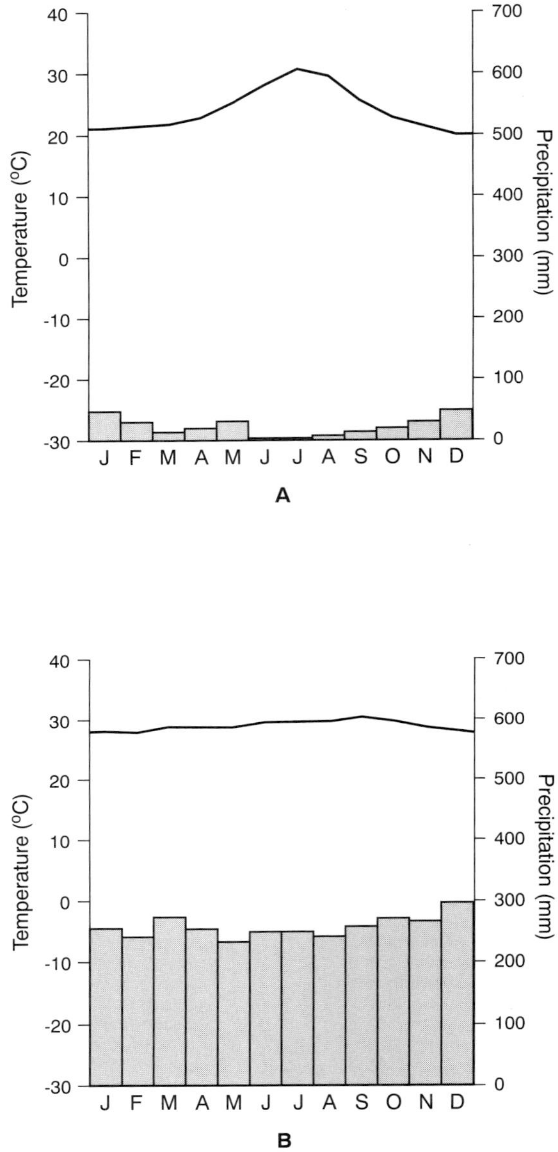

FIGURE 3.3 Two climatic graphs

EXTENSION TASKS

4 Look at the sketch of the Hot Desert landscape shown as Figure 3.4.

(a) Give two problems facing farmers in this landscape. (2)

(b) Explain why settlement is possible at the oasis. (2)

(c) Give two reasons why tourists might want to visit this area. (2)

(6)

FIGURE 3.4 A Hot Desert landscape

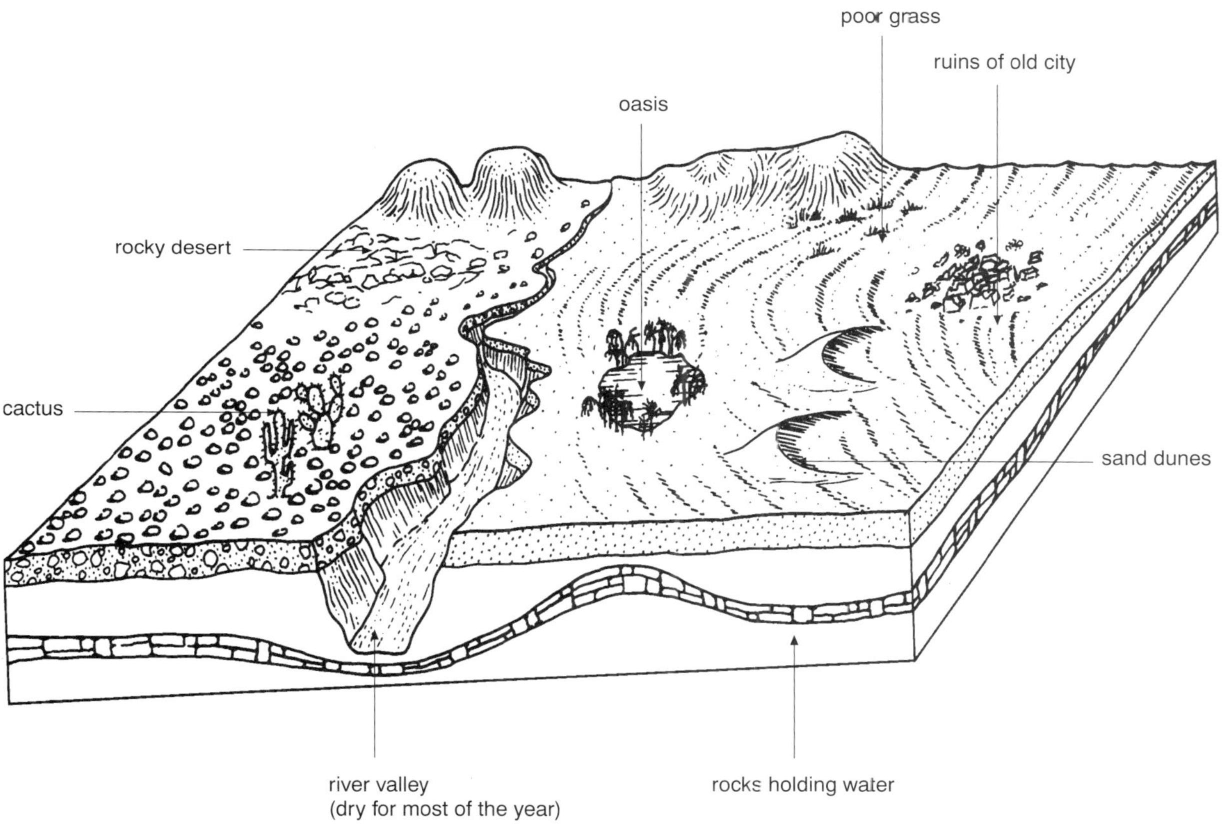

5 Figure 3.5 shows four tables of climatic statistics.

(a) Name the climatic region which each table represents. State the features which helped you identify these climatic regions. (8)

(b) Choose two of these climatic regions and explain their main features. (4)

(12)

TOTAL NUMBER OF MARKS **36**

TABLE A	J	F	M	A	M	J	J	A	S	O	N	D
Temperature (°C)	16	19	25	28	32	33	33	32	31	27	22	17
Rainfall (mm)	0	0	0	0	0	0	3	15	8	0	0	0

TABLE B	J	F	M	A	M	J	J	A	S	O	N	D
Temperature (°C)	25	26	27	27	26	25	24	24	24	25	26	26
Rainfall (mm)	66	165	254	220	432	472	250	236	490	627	269	165

TABLE C	J	F	M	A	M	J	J	A	S	O	N	D
Temperature (°C)	9	10	12	15	20	25	28	27	24	19	15	11
Rainfall (mm)	60	36	38	23	23	15	6	7	15	51	56	71

TABLE D	J	F	M	A	M	J	J	A	S	O	N	D
Temperature (°C)	−20	−18	−14	−10	−8	−6	4	7	8	2	−4	−12
Rainfall (mm)	10	12	15	15	20	25	28	22	20	12	10	8

FIGURE 3.5 Four tables of climatic statistics

4

The physical environment and its effect on human activities

Key Idea

The physical environment offers a range of possibilities for, and limitations on, human activities.

CORE QUESTIONS

1 Study the photograph of the Alpine valley shown as Figure 4.1.

(a) Give one piece of evidence which suggests that this area has been shaped by ice. (1)

(b) State two ways in which the floor of the valley is being used. (1)

(c) State two ways in which the lower slopes of the mountains can be used. (2)

(d) State two ways in which the upper slopes of the mountains can be used. (2)

(6)

FIGURE 4.1 An Alpine valley

2 Figure 4.2 shows weather conditions in Scotland.

Explain why the weather might affect:

(a) drivers in north Scotland; (2)

(b) air travellers in west Scotland; (2)

(c) farmers in south Scotland. (2)

(6)

FIGURE 4.2 Weather conditions in Scotland

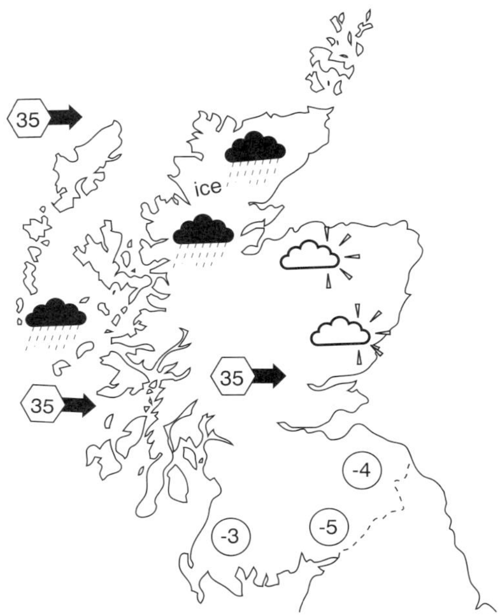

3 Study Figures 4.3A and 4.3B which provide information about Cascais, a holiday resort on the Estoril Coast of Portugal.

(a) Describe the features of the climate which help to attract people to Cascais. (4)

(b) Explain why features of the coastal landscape would also help to attract people to Cascais. (4)

FIGURE 4.3A The coastal landscape at Cascais

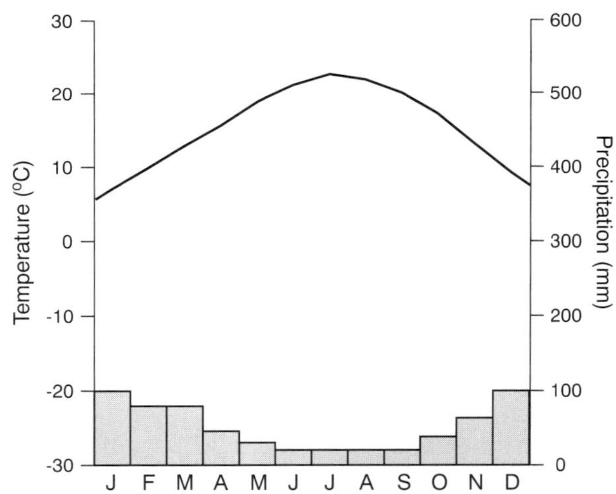

FIGURE 4.3B The climate of Cascais

(c) Apart from coastal areas, describe two other types of landscape which are popular with tourists. Outline the sort of activities which can be carried out on each landscape. (4)

(12)

4 Figure 4.4 shows the route of the M80 motorway.

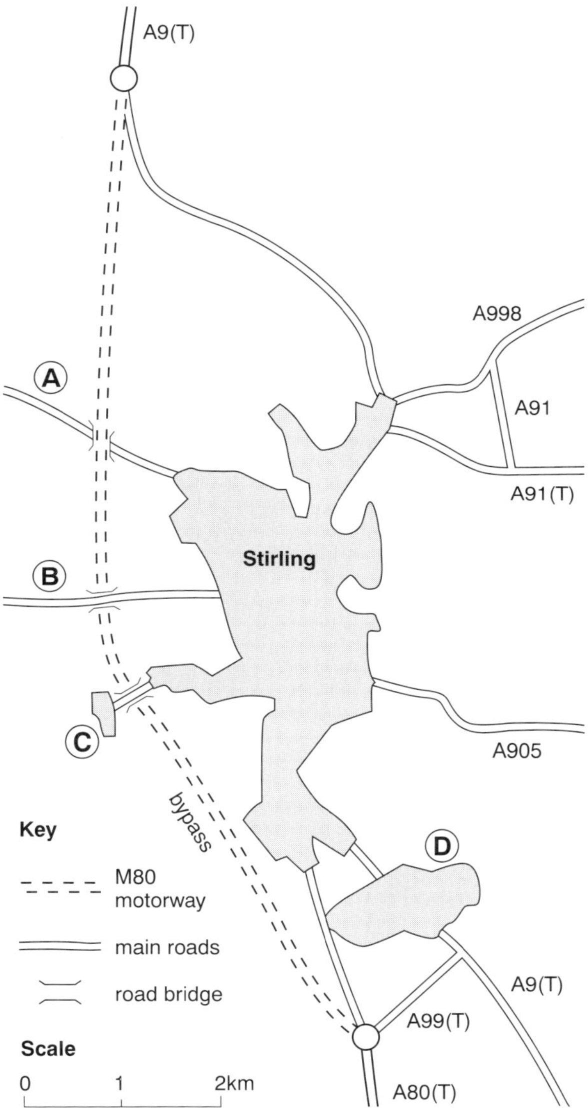

FIGURE 4.4 The route of the M80 motorway

(a) Use the Ordnance Survey map on the inside back cover to help you name:

i. the trunk road at **A**
ii. the main road at **B**
iii. the settlement at **C**
iv. the settlement at **D**. (4)

(b) The M80 was built to bypass Stirling. Use the Ordnance Survey map on the inside back cover to identify one physical obstacle which had to be overcome by the motorway builders. (1)

(c) Explain how the physical obstacle you stated for **(b)** was overcome. (1)

(6)

EXTENSION TASKS

5 Figure 4.5 shows a cross-section which runs from GR 774947 to GR 809981 on the Ordnance Survey map on the inside back cover. Six areas of land use have been identified with the letters **A** to **F**.

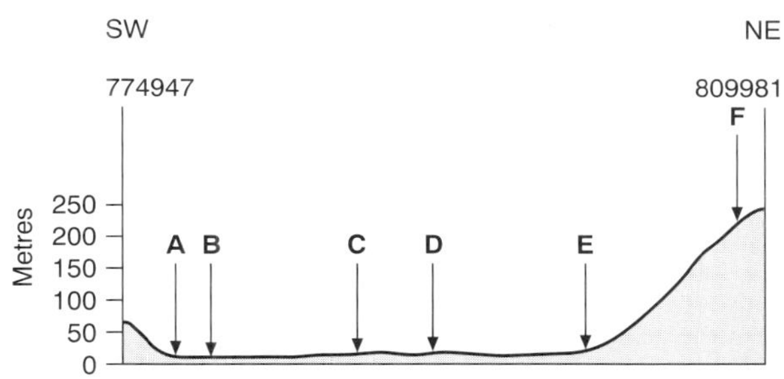

FIGURE 4.5 A cross-section

(a) Which letter marks the position of:

i. the A9 trunk road
ii. the railway
iii. woodland
iv. the M9 motorway
v. the river
vi. the A84 trunk road? (3)

(b) Choose one of the land uses you identified in **(a)** and explain its location. (3)

(6)

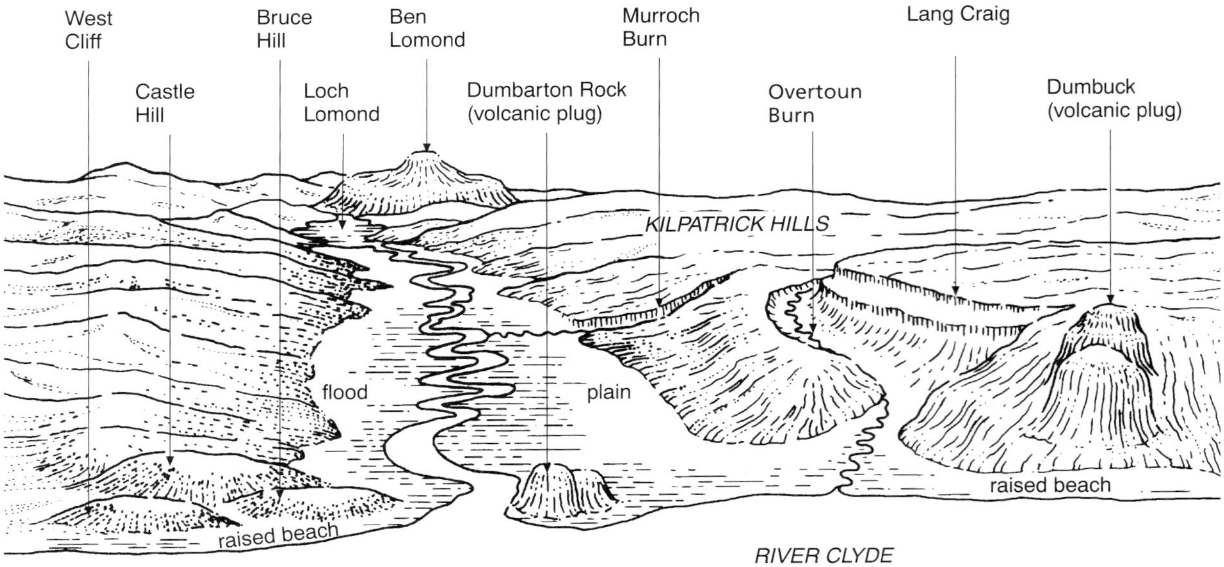

FIGURE 4.6 A landscape in central Scotland

6 Study the sketch of the landscape in Figure 4.6.

What possibilities and limitations are provided by a landscape such as this? (6)

(6)

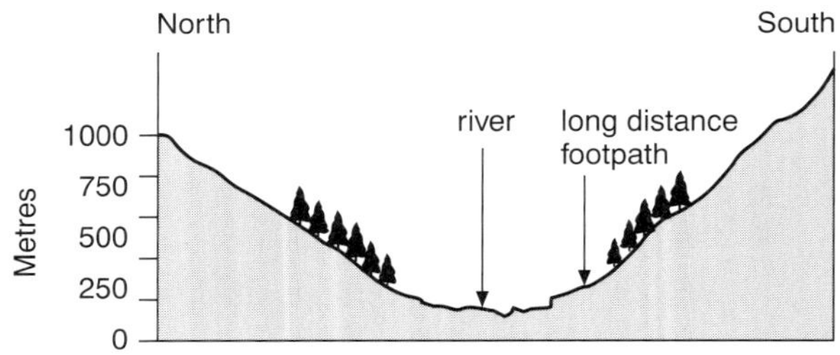

Relief	upper slopes	lower slopes	Valley floor	lower slopes	upper slopes
Soil	thin and infertile	peat	alluvial	peat	thin and infertile
Land use	sheep farming	forestry	crops and improved pasture; settlements	forestry	sheep farming

FIGURE 4.7 A transect through a glaciated valley

7 Look at Figure 4.7 which shows a transect through a glaciated valley.

(a) Describe and explain the location of:
 i. the cultivated land
 ii. the forests
 iii. the settlements
 iv. the long distance footpath. (8)

(b) Make your own transect of the valley and then mark in suitable sites for each of the following:
 i. an outdoor sports centre for school pupils
 ii. a tourist information centre.

Give reasons for each choice. (4)

(12)

TOTAL NUMBER OF MARKS **54**

5

Competition for the use of rural landscapes

Key Idea **There are many competing demands for the use of rural landscapes.**

CORE QUESTIONS

1 Look at Figure 5.1 which shows a landscape in the Highlands of Scotland.

(a) List three different uses of this landscape. (3)

(b) Why might the people at **A** come into conflict with the people at **B**? (3)

(c) Who might object to the idea of a ski development at **C**?
Outline what their objections might be. (3)

(d) Who might support the idea of a ski development at **C**?
Give reasons for their support of the development. (3)

(12)

FIGURE 5.1 A landscape in the Highlands of Scotland

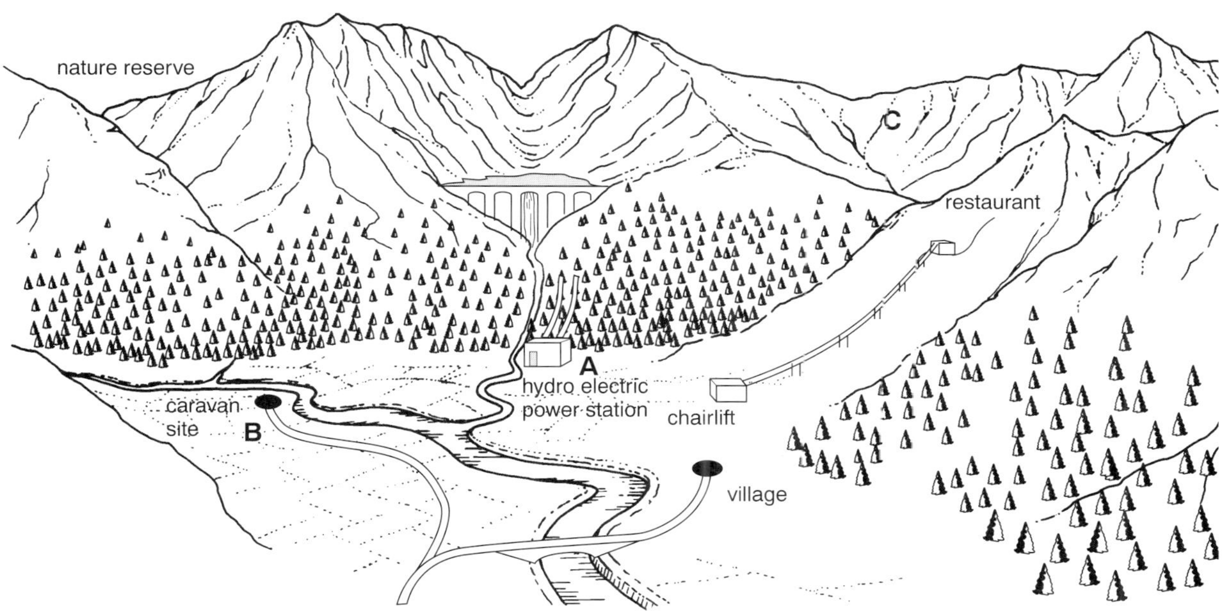

FIGURE 5.2A A hydro-electric power scheme in Perthshire

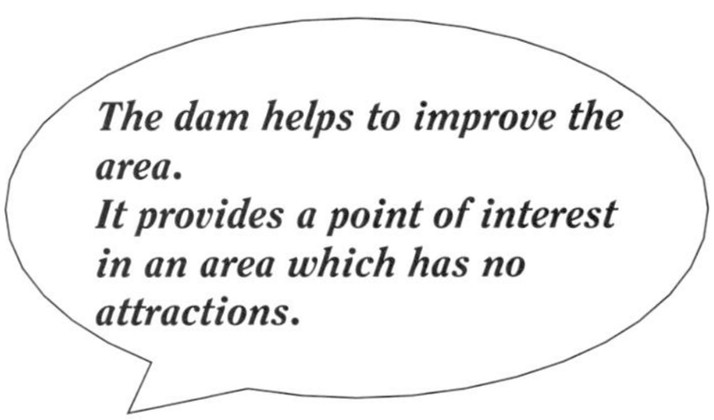

A worker for the construction company which built the dam.

FIGURE 5.2B One person's opinion of the HEP scheme

2 Figure 5.2A shows a hydro-electric power scheme in Perthshire. Figure 5.2B is one person's opinion of the scheme.

(a) Who might have objected to this scheme being built?
Suggest reasons for their objections. (4)

(b) Why is the statement in Figure 5.2B an example of bias? (2)

(6)

EXTENSION TASKS

3 Study Figure 5.3 which shows a plan for a quarry at the edge of a town.

(a) Outline the economic benefits a quarry might bring to the town. (3)

(b) Suggest the environmental problems which might arise if a quarry is created. (3)

(6)

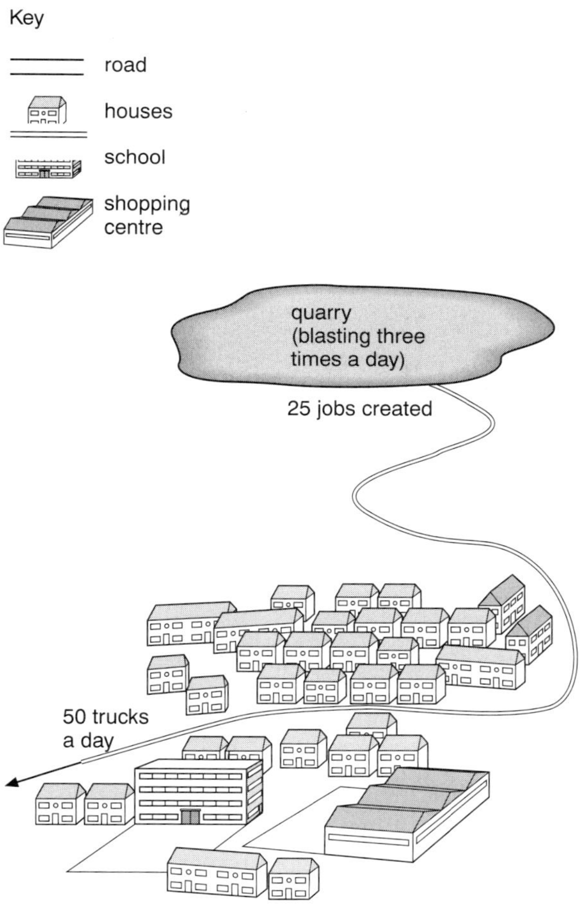

FIGURE 5.3 Plan for a quarry at the edge of a town

4 Figure 5.4 shows land and wildlife resou in the Cairngorm Mountains.

- long snow season
- spectacular scenery
- herds of deer
- rare birds and plants
- rivers and lochs
- steep corries and cliffs
- ancient woods of pine and birch

FIGURE 5.4 Land and wildlife resources in the Cairngorm Mountains

(a) What makes the Cairngorm Mountains a suitable area for recreation and tourism? (3)

(b) What impact might recreation and tourism have on a fragile landscape like the Cairngorms? (3)

(6)

5 Look at Figure 5.5 which shows part of the Lake District National Park.

(a) State what is meant by a 'national park'. (2)

(b) Suggest reasons why the area shown in the photograph has been included in a national park. (4)

(c) Outline the effect that national park rules have on:

i. tourists
ii. local farms
iii. local industries. (6)

(12)

TOTAL NUMBER OF MARKS **42**

FIGURE 5.5 Part of the Lake District National Park

6
Environmental issues

Key Idea **The physical environment is a resource which has to be used with care and its management is a global issue.**

CORE QUESTIONS

1 Look at Figure 6.1 which shows water pollution.

(a) List three ways in which the sea is being polluted. (3)

(b) Describe how pollution of the sea will affect:

i. the fishing village at **A**
ii. the houses at **B**
iii. the caravan site at **C**. (3)

(6)

FIGURE 6.1 Water pollution

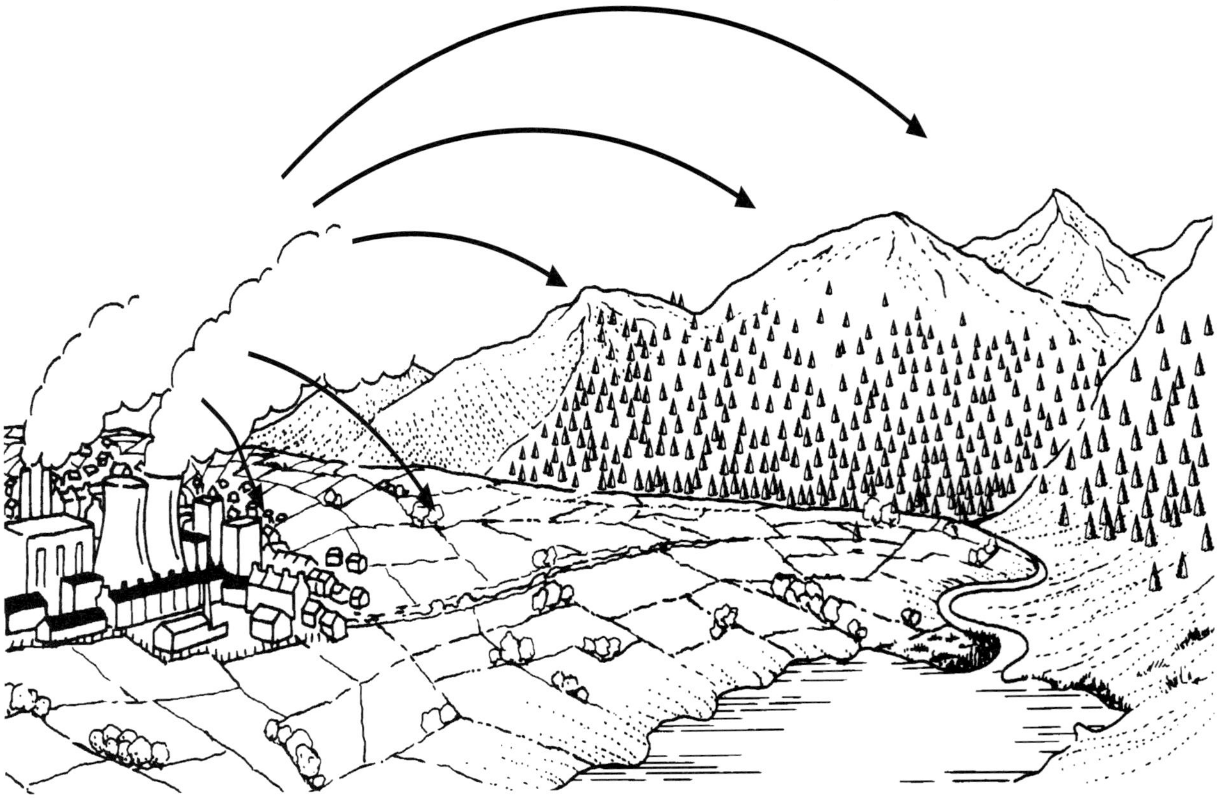

Urban areas	Farming areas	Rivers and lakes	Mountain areas
buildings and statues are eroded	crop outputs are reduced	fish are poisoned	trees are killed

FIGURE 6.2 The causes and effects of acid rain

2 Figure 6.2 shows the causes and effects of acid rain.

(a) State the:

i. source of the pollution

ii. the effect of the acid rain on the mountains and moorlands. (4)

(b) What can governments do to reduce acid rain? (2)

(6)

EXTENSION TASKS

3 Study Figure 6.3 which shows four possible solutions to the problem of spreading deserts.
Explain how each solution might be able to slow down the spread of deserts. (6)

(6)

FIGURE 6.3 Some possible solutions to the problem of spreading deserts

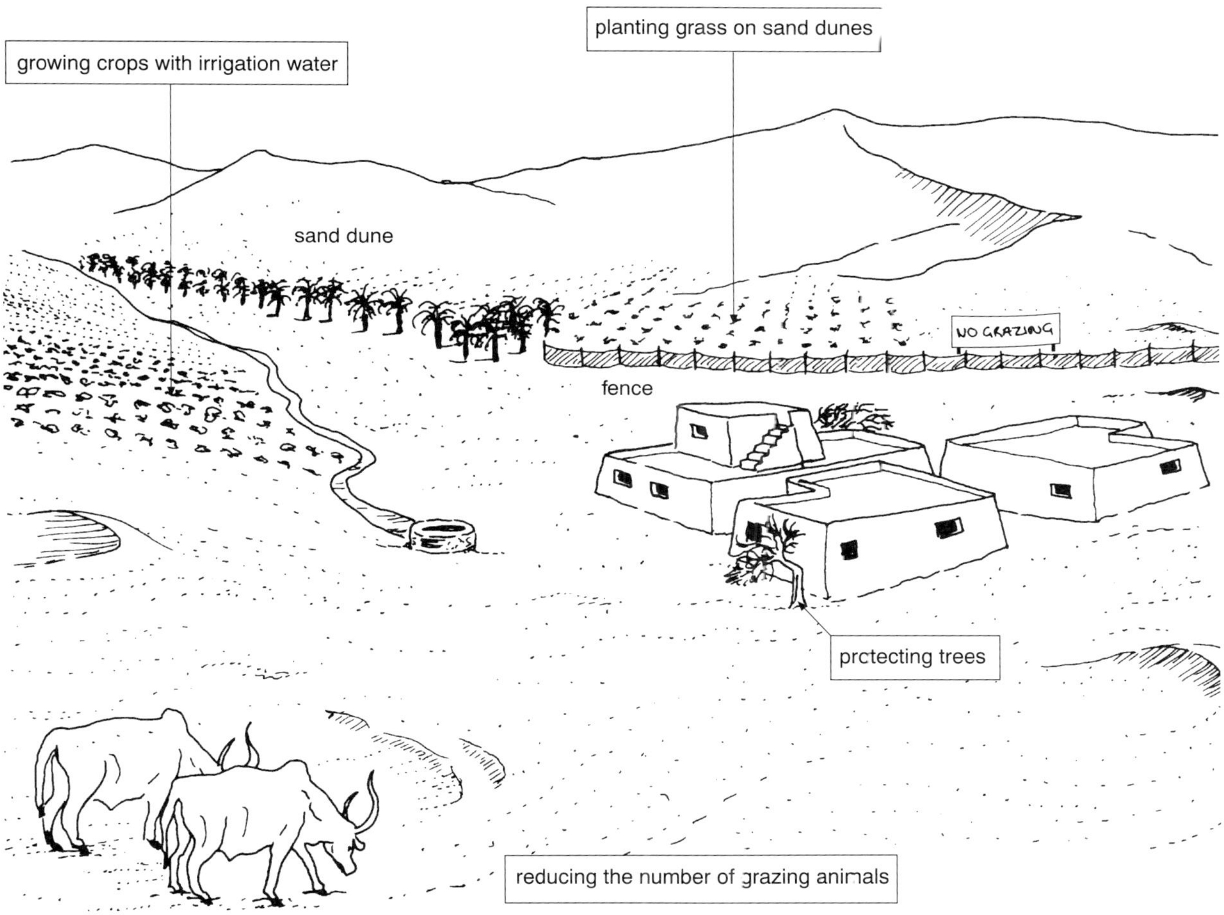

4 Figure 6.4 shows an Equatorial Rainforest landscape before and after deforestation.

(a) Describe the changes which have taken place. (4)

(b) Outline the problems which are likely to arise from the destruction of the rainforest. (6)

(c) In spite of the problems why do many countries cut down large areas of rainforests? (2)

(12)

TOTAL NUMBER OF MARKS **30**

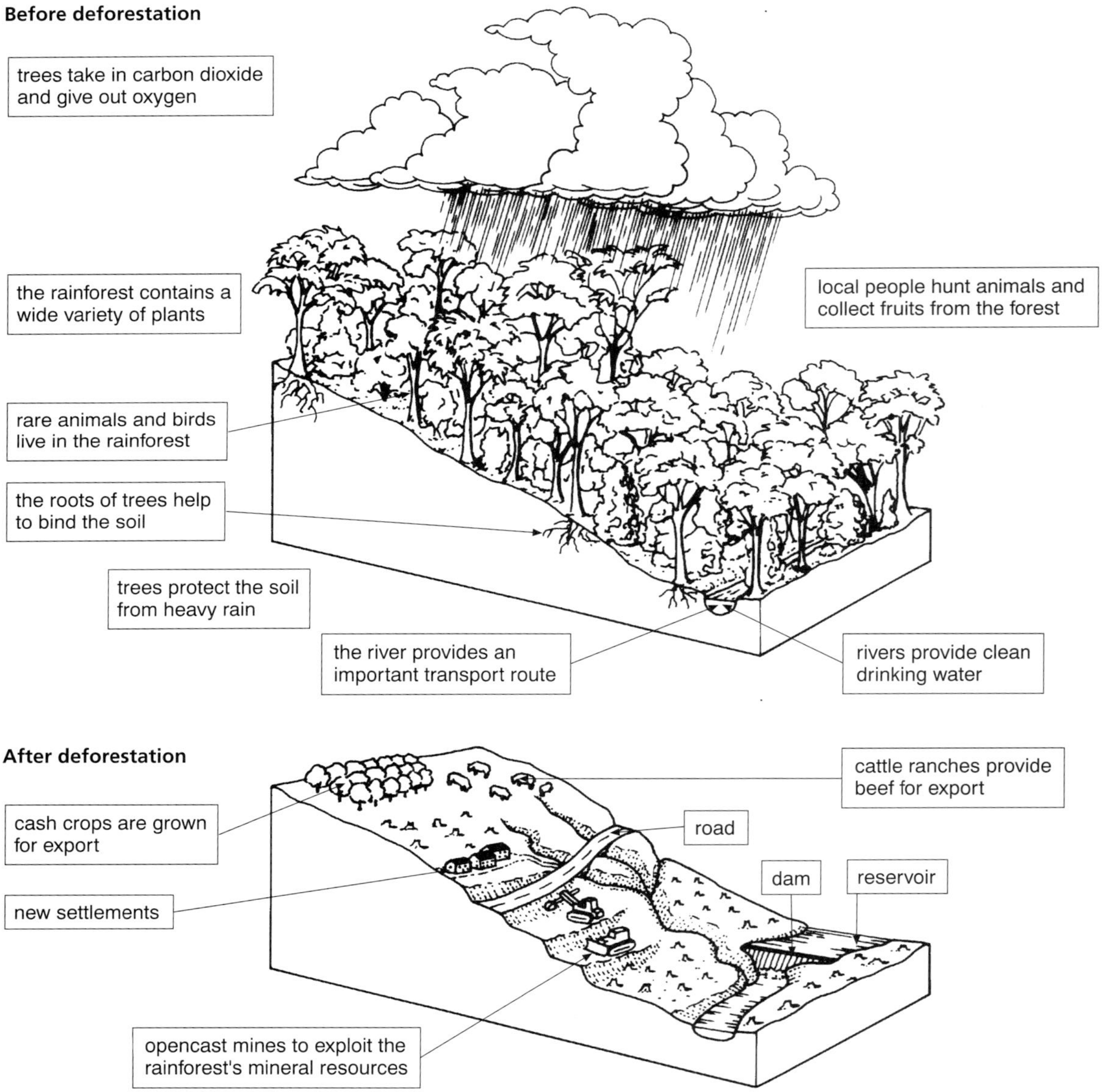

FIGURE 6.4 An Equatorial Rainforest landscape before and after deforestation

7

Characteristics of settlements

Key Idea **Settlements have many common characteristics relating to size, situation and function.**

CORE QUESTIONS

1 Look at Figure 7.1 which shows the sites of three settlements.

(a) Describe the site of the settlement at **A**. (2)

(b) Why do you think **B** provided a good site for a castle? (2)

(c) Why do you think the settlement at **C** has not become a large settlement? (2)

(6)

FIGURE 7.1 The sites of three settlements

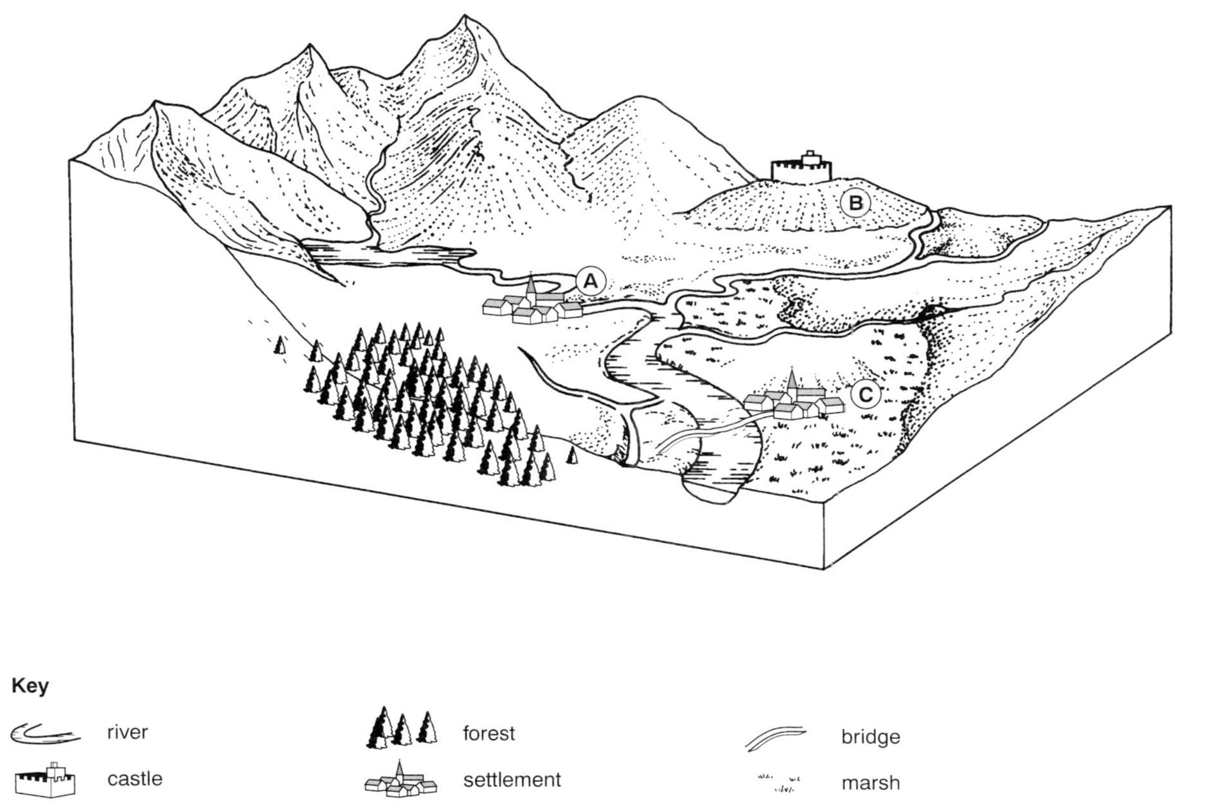

Rural-urban fringe	Suburb	Inner city	City centre
commuter village	new residential area with detached and semi-detached houses	old houses and old factories being replaced by new houses	the central business district, offices, department stores, entertainment and transport facilities
low population density	medium population density	very high population density	low population density

FIGURE 7.2A A model of urban land use

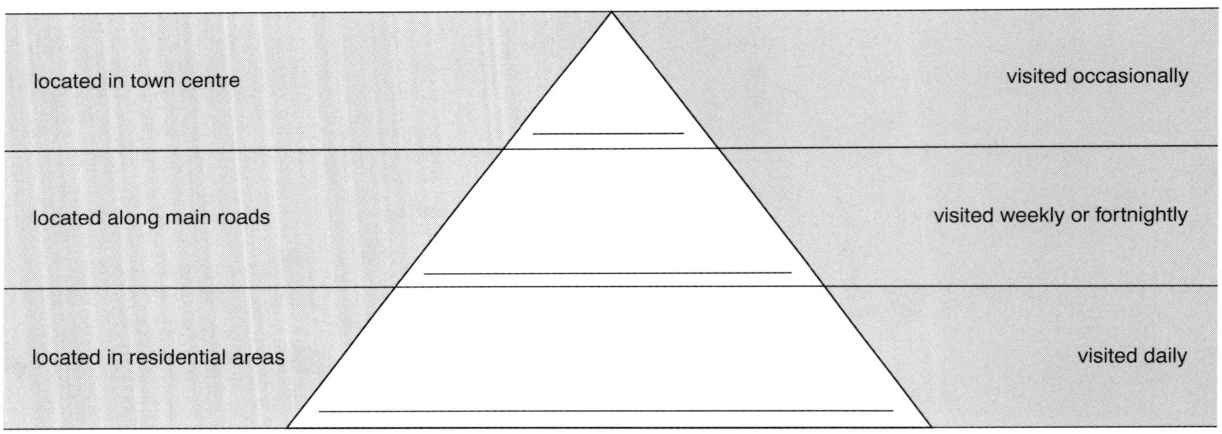

FIGURE 7.2B The hierarchy of shops in a city

2 **(a)** Figure 7.2A shows a model of urban land use.
Describe the changes in land use from the city centre to the rural-urban fringe. (4)

(b) Suggest reasons for the changes in population density from the city centre to the rural-urban fringe. (4)

(c) Figure 7.2B shows the hierarchy of shops in a city.
Copy the diagram and then complete it by writing the following terms in the correct places:

small corner shops
large department stores
shopping centres (4)

(12)

EXTENSION TASKS

3 Study Figure 7.3 which shows the number of services in different settlements.

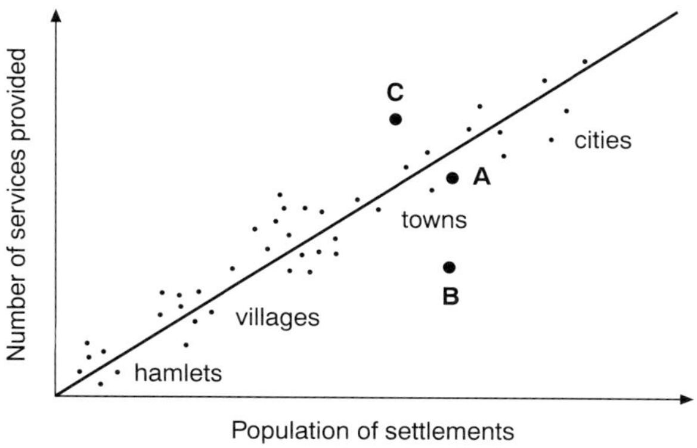

FIGURE 7.3 Services and settlements

(a) Give two examples of services which are normally found in towns and cities but not in hamlets and villages. (2)

(b) Name the town (**A**, **B** or **C**) which has more services than the other towns. Suggest a reason why this town has more services than the other towns. (2)

(c) Name the town (**A**, **B** or **C**) which has fewer services than the other towns. Suggest a reason why this town has fewer services than the other towns. (2)

(d) State the meaning of the term 'sphere of influence' and outline the steps you would take to find out the sphere of influence of a market town. (6)

(12)

4 Figure 7.4 shows the location of Glasgow.

(a) Describe the physical factors which make Glasgow an important route centre. (4)

(b) What functions are usually associated with route centres? (2)

(6)

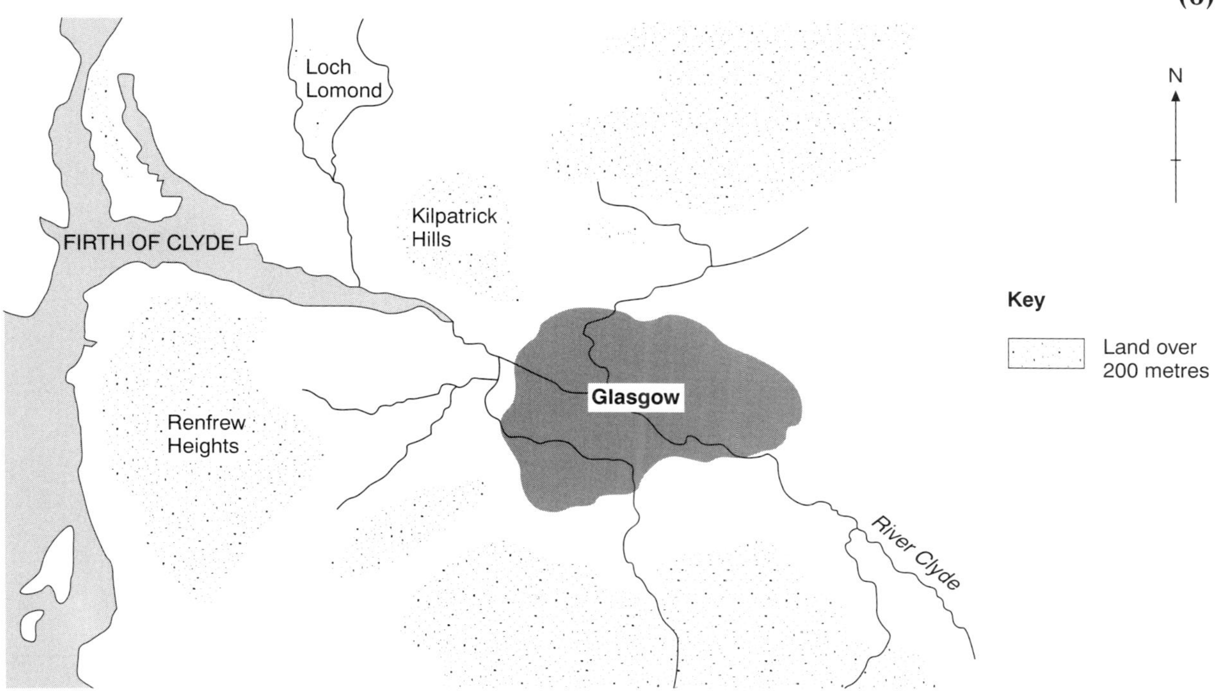

FIGURE 7.4 The location of Glasgow

5 Look at the Ordnance Survey map of Stirling on the inside back cover.

(a) Describe the site of Stirling. (3)

(b) Outline the ways in which Stirling's site has influenced the town's growth. (3)

(c) 'The River Forth is Stirling's reason for existence.'
Why do you think the River Forth has been so important to the development of Stirling? (3)

(d) Which grid square has the town centre of Stirling?
Give two pieces of map evidence to support your choice. (2)

(e) What map evidence suggests that Stirling is a centre for tourism?
Give two pieces of evidence. (1)

(12)

TOTAL NUMBER OF MARKS **48**

8 Urban change

Key Idea **Urban settlements have dynamic patterns relating to their size, form and function.**

CORE QUESTIONS

1 Study Figure 8.1 which shows a model of a new town.

(a) Describe the location of:
  i. the industrial estates
  ii. the town centre
  iii. the recreation areas. (3)

(b) Give reasons for the location of either the industrial estates or the town centre. (3)

(6)

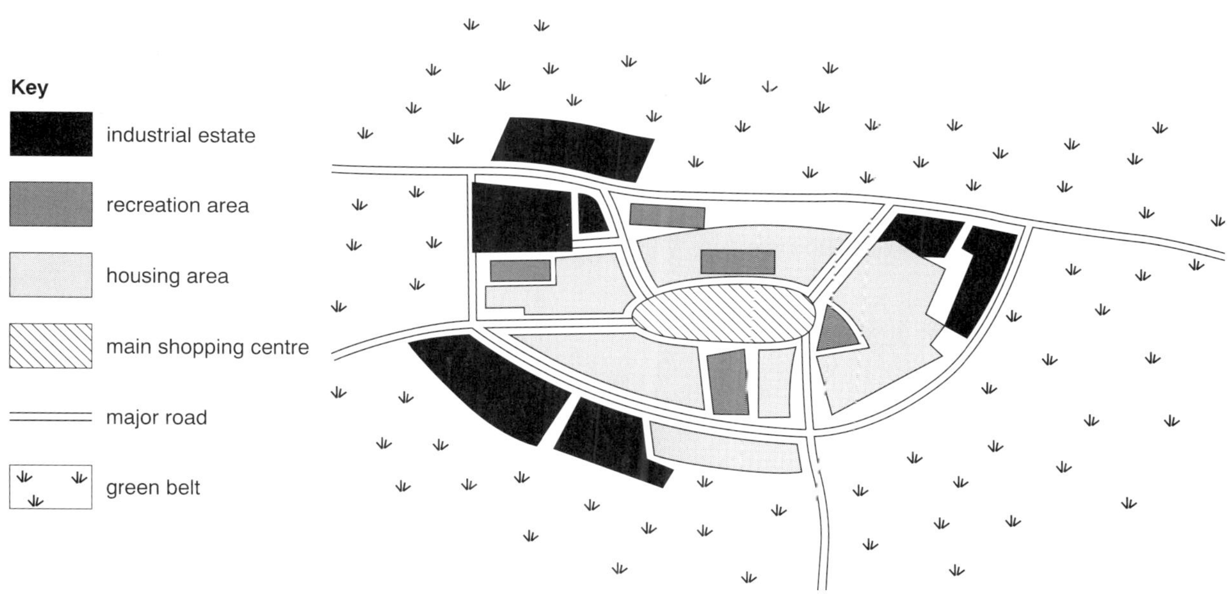

FIGURE 8.1 A model of a new town

FIGURE 8.2 Land use at the edge of Stirling

2 Figure 8.2 shows land use at the edge of Stirling.

(a) State three ways in which the land is being used at the edge of Stirling. (3)

(b) There are many pressures on the countryside at the edges of towns and cities.
What are the advantages and disadvantages of building on the countryside at the edges of towns and cities? (4)

(c) Part of Figure 8.2 is a 'green belt'.
State the meaning of the term 'green belt' and give two reasons why green belts are found at the edges of towns and cities. (3)

(d) Many large warehouses and shops are being built on the edges of towns and cities. Suggest reasons why. (2)

(12)

EXTENSION TASKS

FIGURE 8.3 Houses in an inner-city area

3 Look at Figure 8.3 which shows houses in an inner-city area.

(a) Outline the problems which are associated with many old houses in inner-city areas. (3)

(b) Explain why many high-rise flats were built to replace old houses in inner-city areas? (2)

(c) Apart from constructing new houses what else can be done to improve old houses in inner-city areas? (1)

(6)

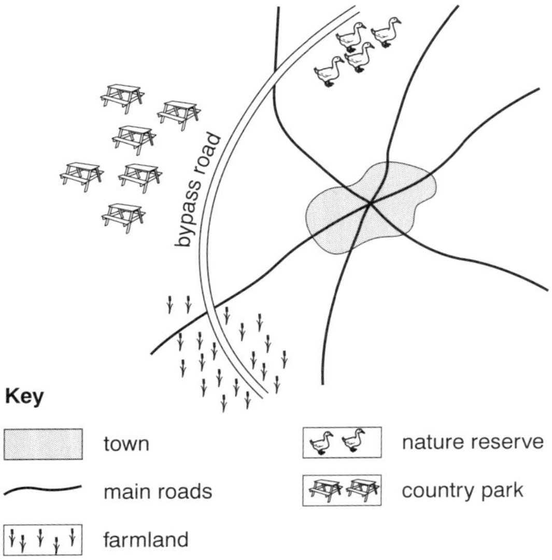

FIGURE 8.4A Plans for a new bypass road

"Car owners can now go anywhere – if they can find somewhere to go."

FIGURE 8.4B One person's view of new roads

4 Figure 8.4A shows a plan for a new bypass road while Figure 8.4B shows one person's view of new roads.

(a) State two groups of people who might object to the new bypass road. Explain why they might object to the plan. (4)

(b) State two groups of people who might support the plan for a new bypass road. Explain why they might support the plan. (4)

(c) Does Figure 8.4B provide a fair viewpoint of new roads? Give reasons for your answer. (4)

(12)

5 (a) Outline in detail one method of finding out how the amount and type of traffic entering a city changes during the course of a day. (3)

(b) Describe, with the help of simple sketch graphs and diagrams, how you would present the results of your investigation. (3)

(6)

TOTAL NUMBER OF MARKS **42**

9 Farming

Key Idea **Farming systems provide food supplies and raw materials.**

CORE QUESTIONS

1 Study Figure 9.1 which shows three maps of Britain.

(a) Answer the following questions:

i. What type of farming is carried out in areas with land above 200 m?

ii. Why is dairying mainly carried out in west Britain?

iii. What type of climate is associated with arable farming? (3)

(b) Apart from relief and climate, what other factors affect the type of farming carried out in an area? Give two different factors. (3)

(6)

FIGURE 9.1 Three maps of Britain

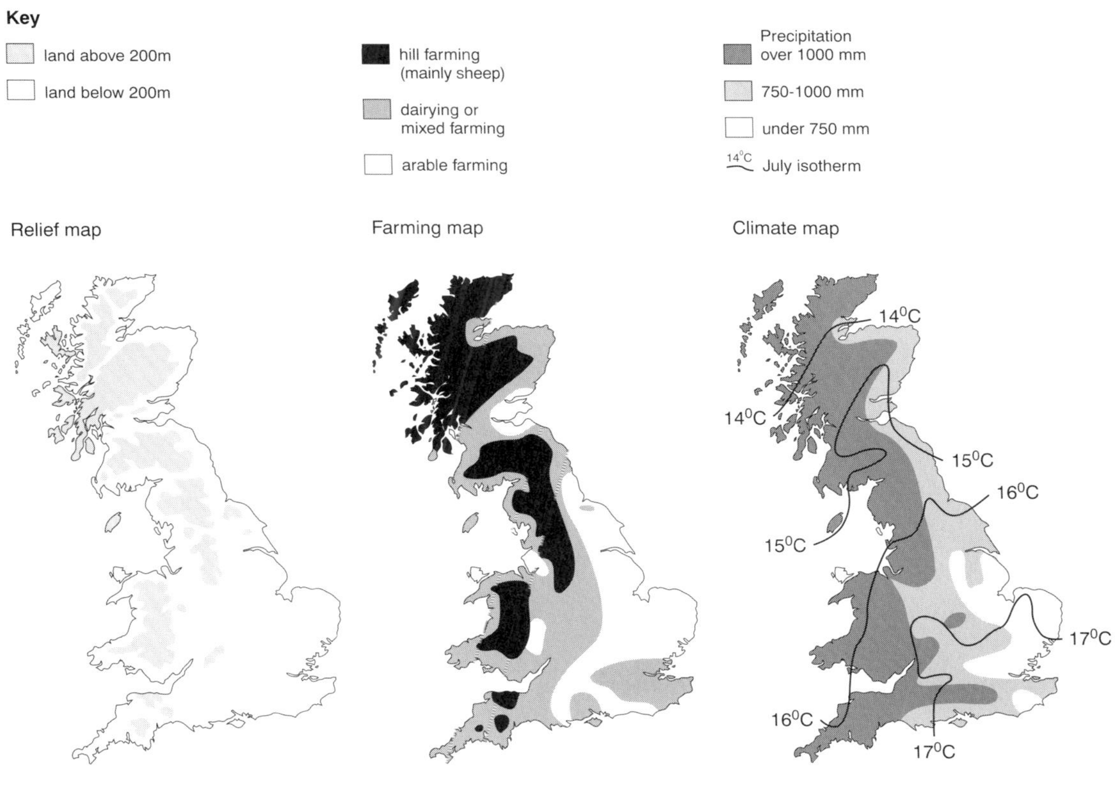

FIGURE 9.2 Problems facing farmers

Problems	Solutions
Wind	Fertilisers
Frost	Embankments
Marshy ground	Shelter belts
Poor soil	Irrigation
Dry soil	Greenhouses
Flooding	Drainage ditches

2 Figure 9.2 shows some of the most common problems facing farmers.

(a) Match each of the problems with the correct solution. (3)

(b) Look at the Ordnance Survey map on the inside back cover. Suggest a possible problem for farmers in grid square:

i. 8194
ii. 8397
iii. 7796. (3)

(6)

3 Figure 9.3 shows a farming area in central Scotland.

(a) Make your own map of this farming area. Mark in a suitable site for each of the following farms:

i. a market garden
ii. an arable farm
iii. a sheep farm. (3)

(b) Explain your choice of location in each case. (3)

(c) Describe one way of investigating how land use in an agricultural region has changed during the past fifty years. Your answer should include a description of the types of graphs and diagrams you would use to present your findings. (6)

(12)

FIGURE 9.3 A farming area in central Scotland

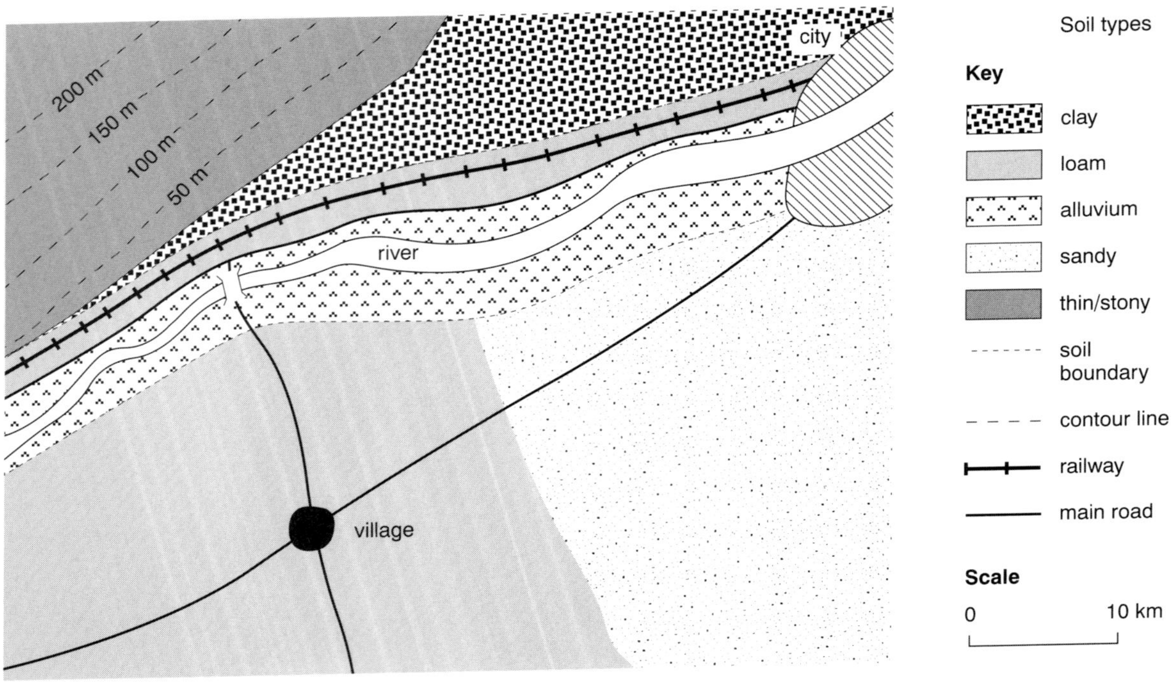

EXTENSION TASKS

4 Look at Figure 9.4 which shows a farm next to Loch Tay in the central Highlands of Scotland.

(a) State three problems facing farmers in this area. (3)

(b) What type of farming is most suited to this area? Give two reasons for your choice. (3)

(6)

FIGURE 9.4 A farm next to Loch Tay in the central Highlands of Scotland

5 Figure 9.5 shows the changes which took place on a Scottish farm between 1945 and 1995.

(a) Describe the changes which have taken place. (4)

(b) Suggest reasons why these changes have taken place. (4)

(c) Who would have benefited from these changes? (2)

(d) Who would have been disadvantaged by these changes? (2)

(12)

	1945	**1995**
size of farm (ha)	135	275
number of workers	16	3
farm machinery		
– tractors	0	3
– combine harvesters	0	2
livestock		
– milk cattle	45	0
– pigs	10	0
crops (ha)		
– wheat	75	175
– barley	25	100
– permanent grass	35	0

FIGURE 9.5 Changes to a Scottish farm

6 Look at Figure 9.6 which shows a large arable farm in east Scotland.

(a) Explain the pattern of land use on this farm. (3)

(b) This farm grows fodder crops. State the meaning of the term 'fodder crop' and give one example of a fodder crop which is being grown on this farm. (2)

(c) This farm also grows cash crops. State the meaning of the term 'cash crop' and give one example of a cash crop which is being grown on this farm. (2)

(d) The farm produces one industrial crop. State the meaning of the term 'industrial crop' and state the industrial crop being produced on this farm. (2)

(e) The farm is run like a business. State what is meant by the term 'agribusiness'. (3)

(12)

FIGURE 9.6 A large arable farm in east Scotland

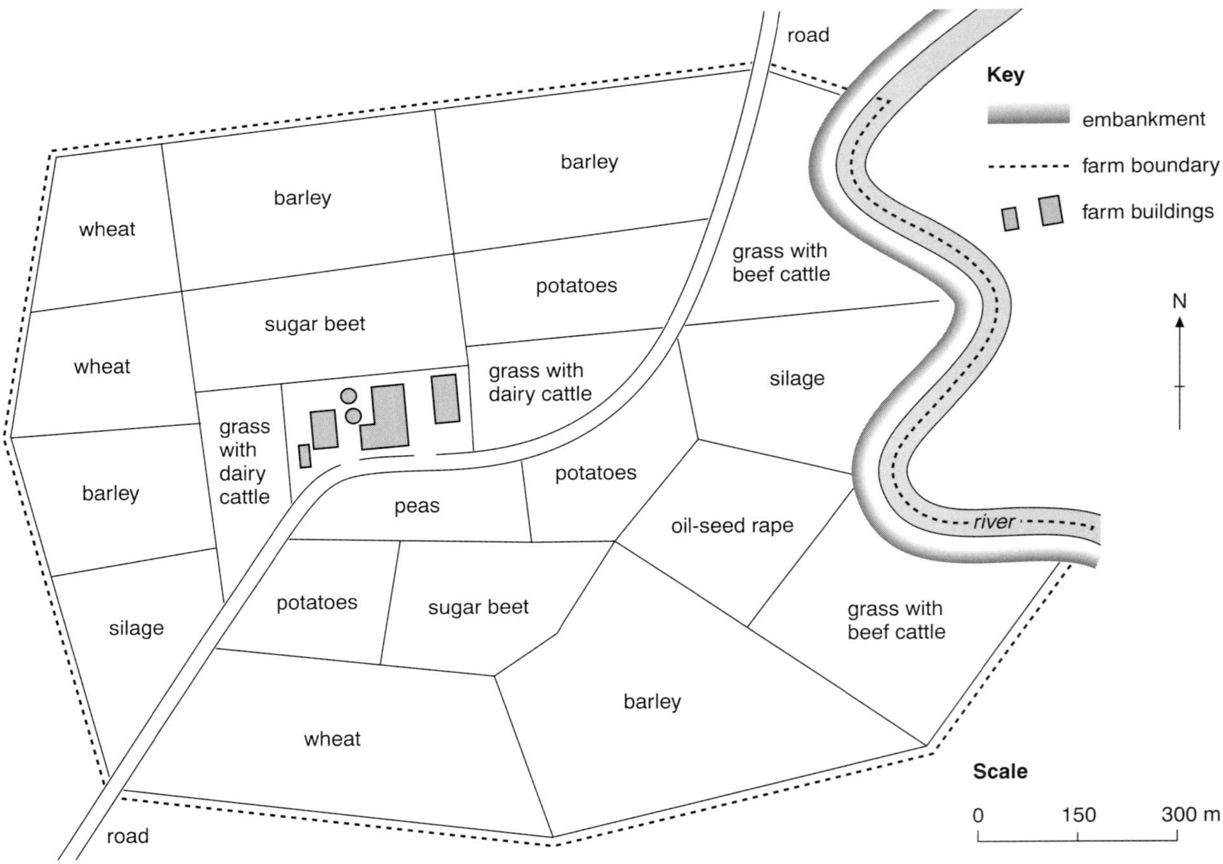

7 Figure 9.7A shows a farming area in Spain while Figure 9.7B shows a model of agricultural land use.

(a) Describe how the farming area is:
i. similar to the model
ii. different from the model. (4)

(b) Suggest ways in which the expanding holiday centre will benefit farming in this area. (2)

(6)

TOTAL NUMBER OF MARKS **60**

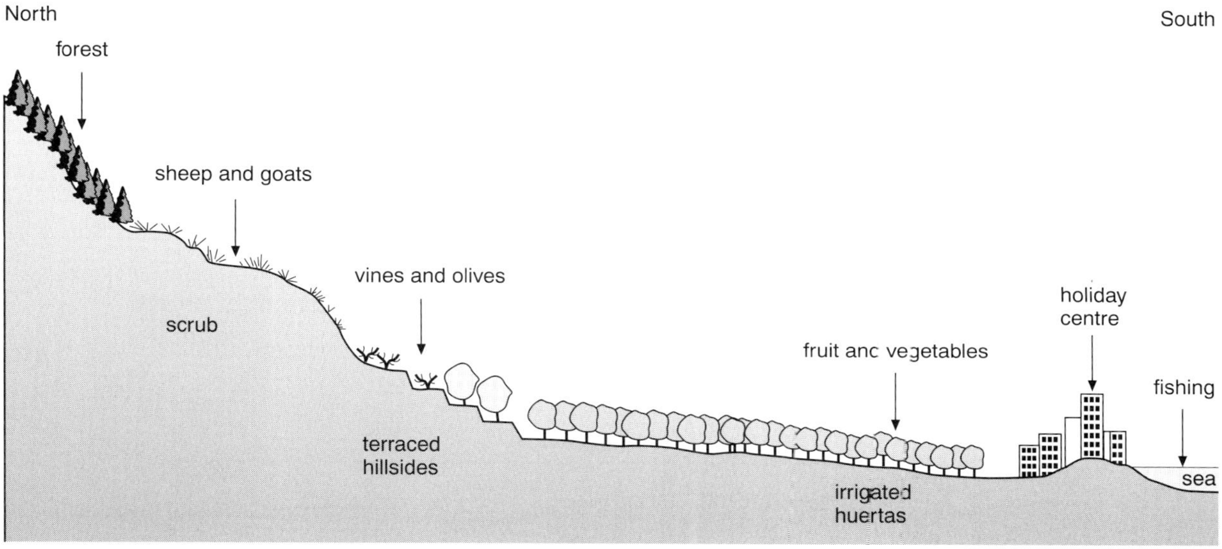

FIGURE 9.7A A farming area in Spain

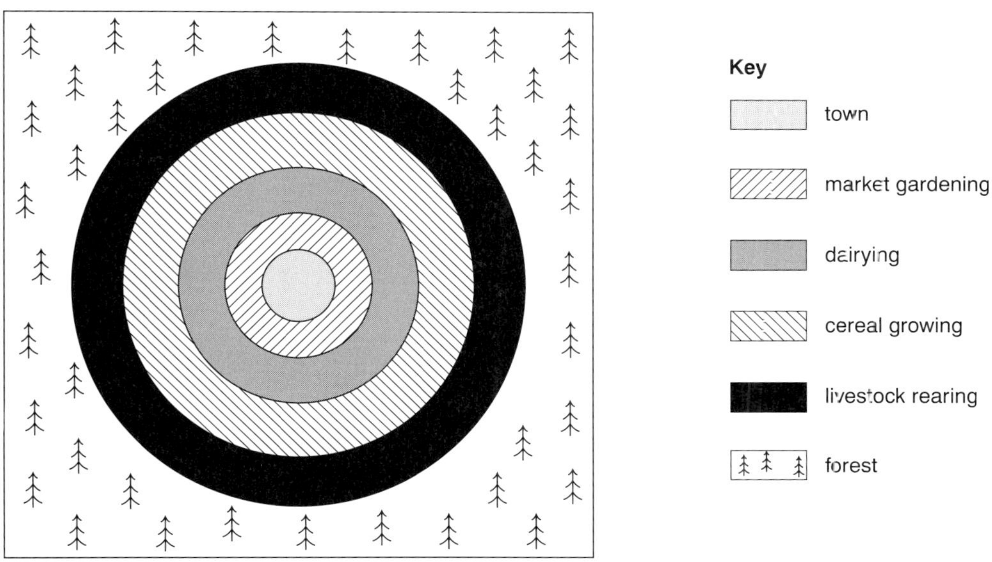

FIGURE 9.7B A model of agricultural land use

10 Industry

Key Idea **The viability of manufacturing industry is affected by a variety of factors.**

CORE QUESTIONS

1 Figure 10.1 shows three possible sites (**A**, **B** or **C**) for an oil refinery.

(a) Choose the best site for the oil refinery and give two reasons for your choice. (3)

(b) Who might object to a new oil refinery in this area?
Explain why they might object. (3)

(6)

FIGURE 10.1 Possible sites for an oil refinery

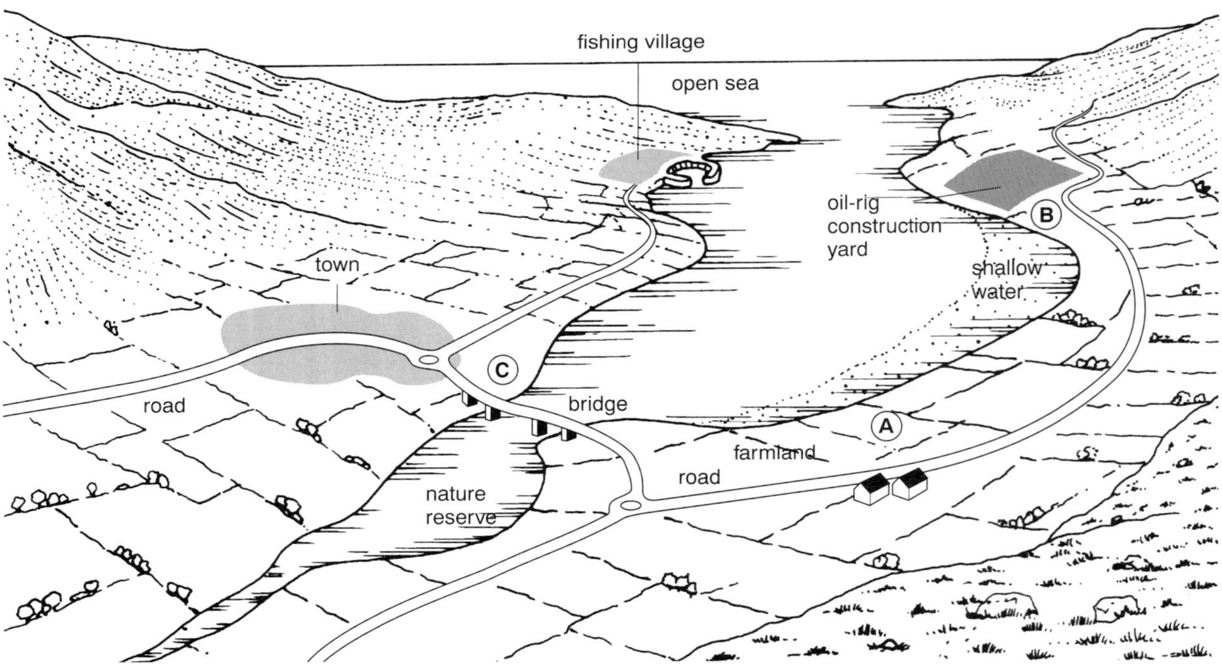

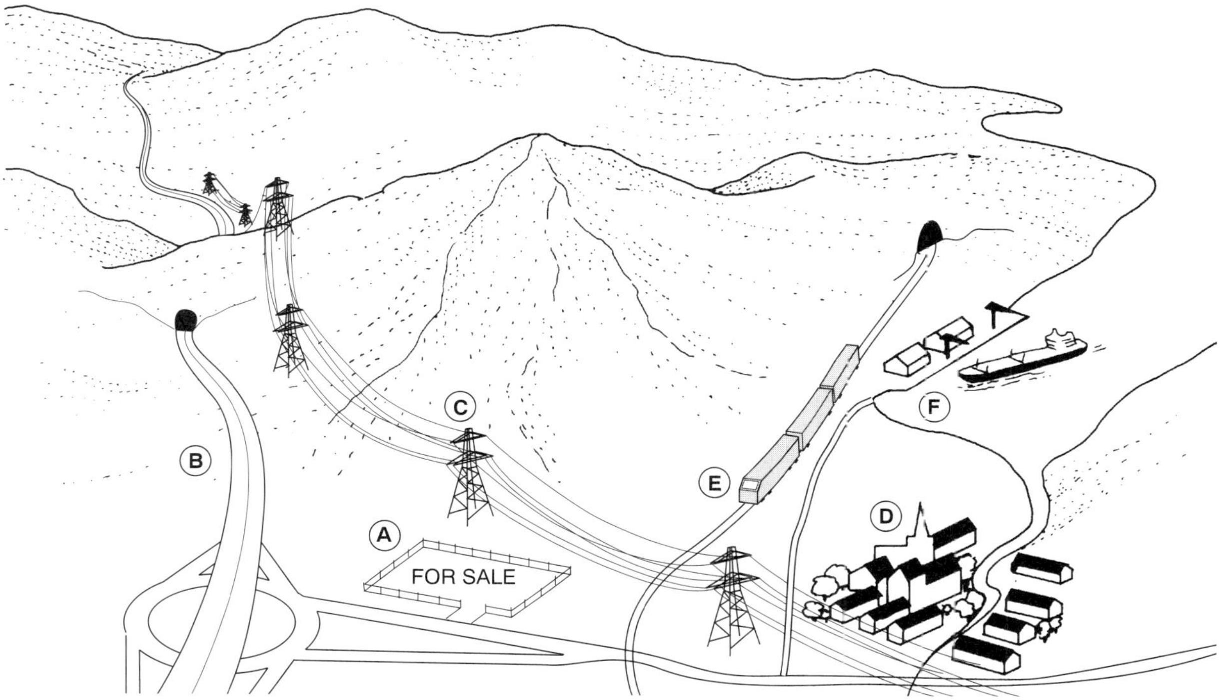

FIGURE 10.2 Important location factors for factories

2 Look at Figure 10.2 which shows some of the location factors (marked **A** to **F**) which are important for factories.

(a) Select four of the factors and explain why they are important. (4)

(b) State two other factors, not shown in Figure 10.2, which also influence the location of factories. (2)

(6)

EXTENSION TASKS

3 Figure 10.3 is a model showing how the location of manufacturing and service industries in the United Kingdom has changed during the past thirty years.

(a) Describe the changes shown by the model. (3)

(b) Give reasons for the changes shown by the model. (3)

(6)

FIGURE 10.3 A model showing changes to the location of manufacturing and service industries

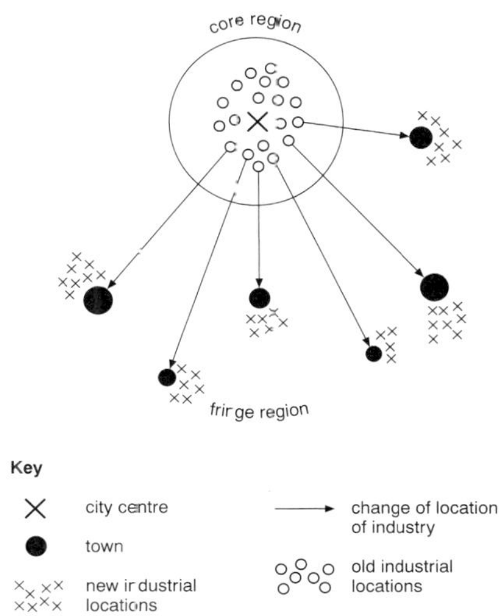

4 Figure 10.4 shows the location of an old and new steelworks.

(a) Explain why site **X** was once a good site for a steelworks. (3)

(b) Explain why site **X** became a difficult site for a steelworks. (3)

(c) Why was the new steelworks built next to the sea? (3)

(d) What problems would have resulted from the closure of the steelworks at **X**? (3)

(12)

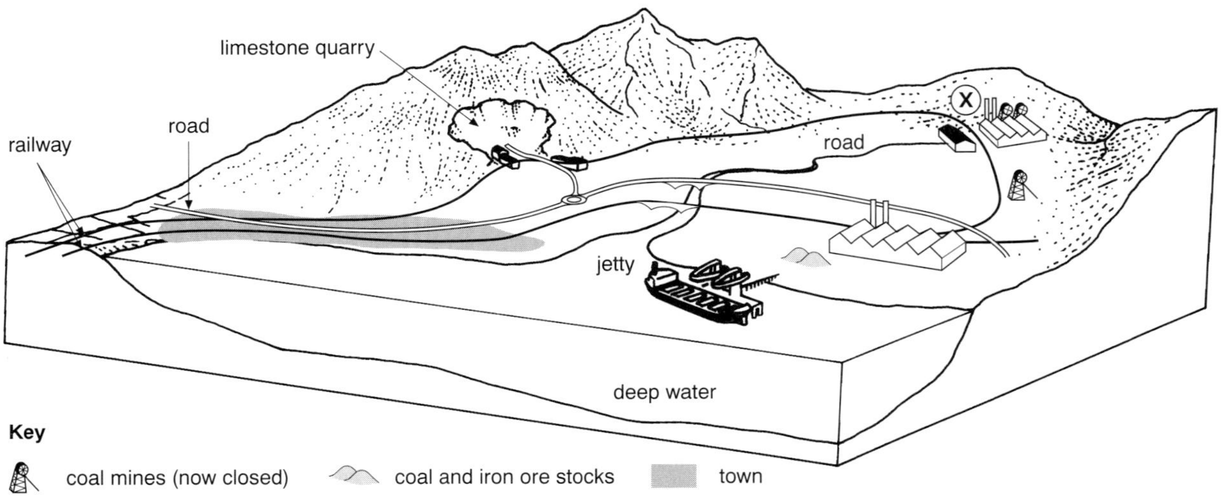

FIGURE 10.4 The location of an old and new steelworks

5 Study Figure 10.5 which shows a new industrial landscape to the north of Stirling.

(a) In what ways does this new industrial landscape differ from an old industrial landscape? (3)

(b) The factories shown in Figure 10.5 include high-tech industries. Give two examples of high-tech industries. (2)

(c) Outline the measures that governments can take to attract high-tech industries to an area. (3)

(d) The industrial landscape in Figure 10.5 can be located at GR 804968 on the Ordnance Survey map on the inside back cover. Use both the photograph and the Ordnance Survey map to help you describe the locational advantages of this site for new industries. (4)

(12)

TOTAL NUMBER OF MARKS **42**

FIGURE 10.5 A new industrial landscape

11 Economic change

Key Idea **Economic change has social and environmental consequences.**

CORE QUESTIONS

1 Figure 11.1 is a pie chart showing employment in a Scottish town.

(a) What percentage of the town's workers are employed in shipbuilding? (1)

(b) Outline the problems which would result if the town's shipyards were to close. (2)

(c) Suggest measures that could be taken to tackle these problems. (3)

(6)

FIGURE 11.1 Employment in a Scottish town

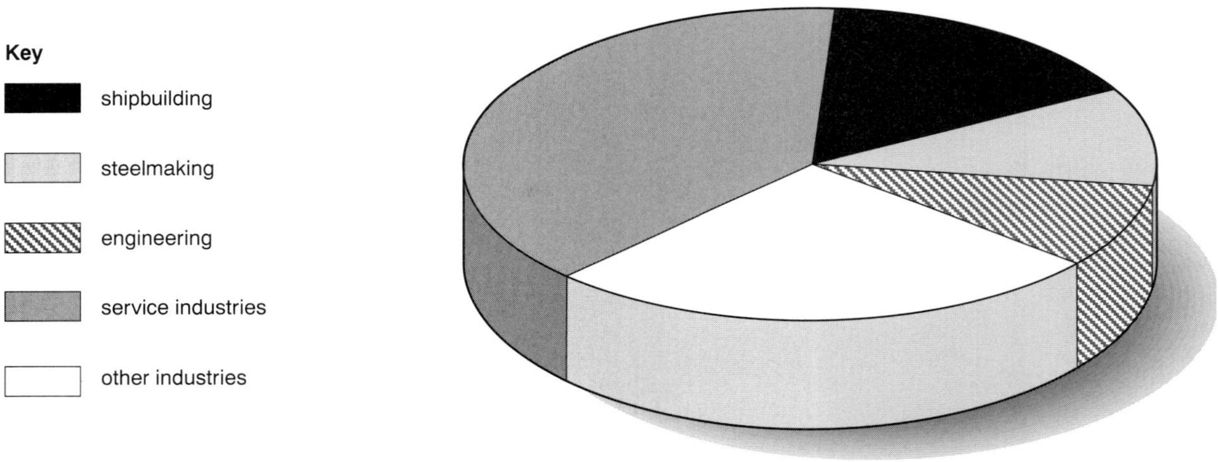

2 Study Figure 11.2 which shows changes to a coastal area.

(a) Describe four changes which have affected this area. (4)

(b) Choose one of the changes and suggest reasons why it occurred. (2)

(6)

FIGURE 11.2 Changes to a coastal area

Before

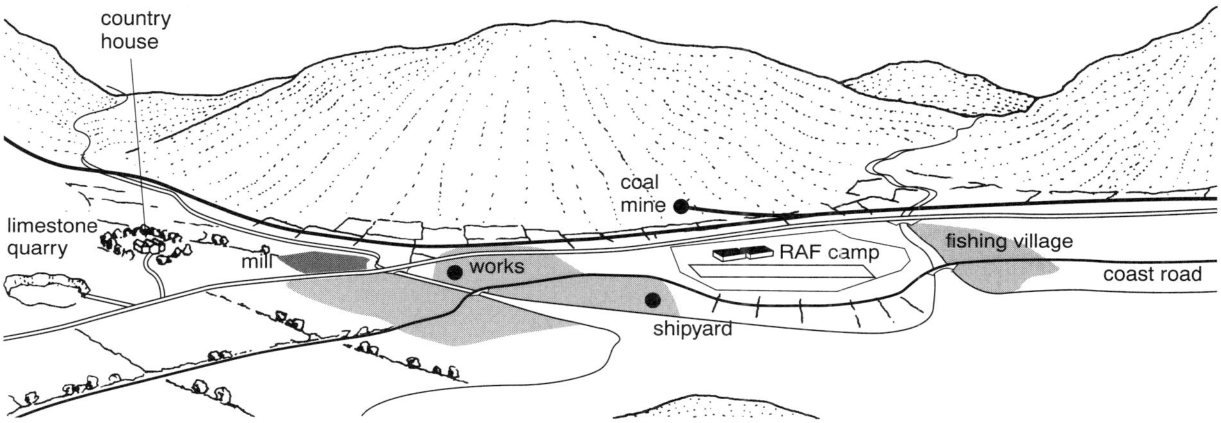

After

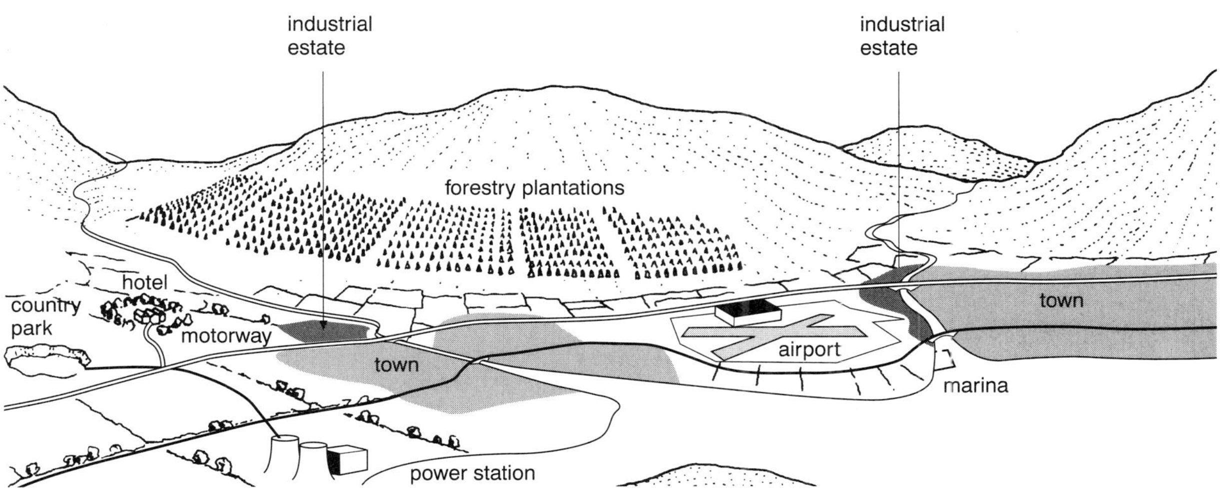

FIGURE 11.3 Derelict land

EXTENSION TASKS

3 Figure 11.3 shows derelict land.

(a) State the meaning of the term 'derelict land'. (2)

(b) Why is the presence of derelict land a problem in many towns and cities? (2)

(c) In spite of the problems, why is derelict land still found in towns and cities? (2)

(6)

4 Look at Figure 11.4 which shows changes to the British coal industry.

(a) Describe the changes shown by the graphs. (3)

(b) Explain why these changes occurred. (3)

(c) Outline the ways these changes would have affected:

i. miners

ii. the economy

iii. the environment. (6)

(12)

TOTAL NUMBER OF MARKS **30**

FIGURE 11.4 Changes to the British coal industry

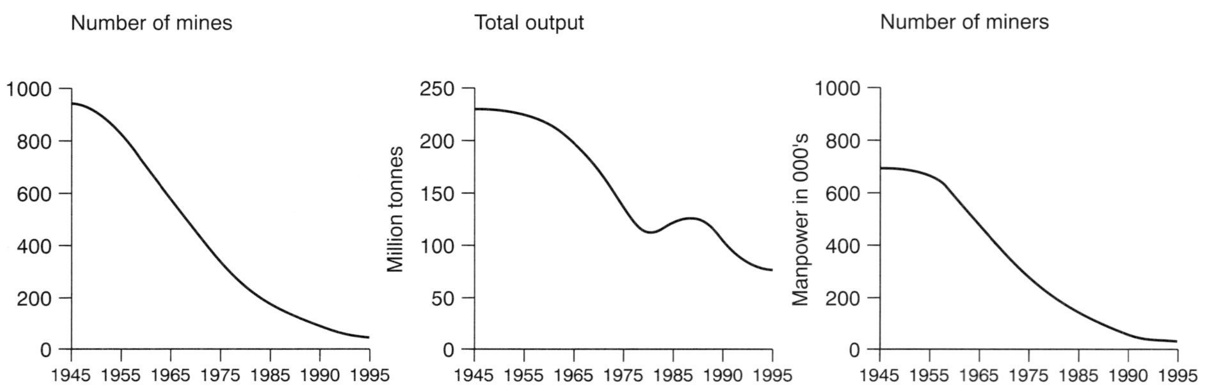

12

Population distribution

Key Idea

Population is unevenly distributed.

CORE QUESTIONS

1 Look at Figure 12.1 which shows four places (**A**, **B**, **C** and **D**) with different population densities.

(a) State which two places have high population densities and which two places have low population densities. (4)

(b) Explain why the population density is high or low in each case. (4)

(c) Apart from the types of places shown in Figure 12.1, what other types of places have high or low population densities? Give two examples of places with high population densities and two examples of places with low population densities. (4)

(12)

FIGURE 12.1 Four places with different population densities

A

B

C

D

2 Figure 12.2 shows the world's largest cities in 1955 and 1995.

(a) State two changes which have taken place. (2)

(b) Suggest reasons why some cities grow faster than others. (4)

(6)

FIGURE 12.2 The world's largest cities in 1955 and 1995

The world's largest cities in 1955

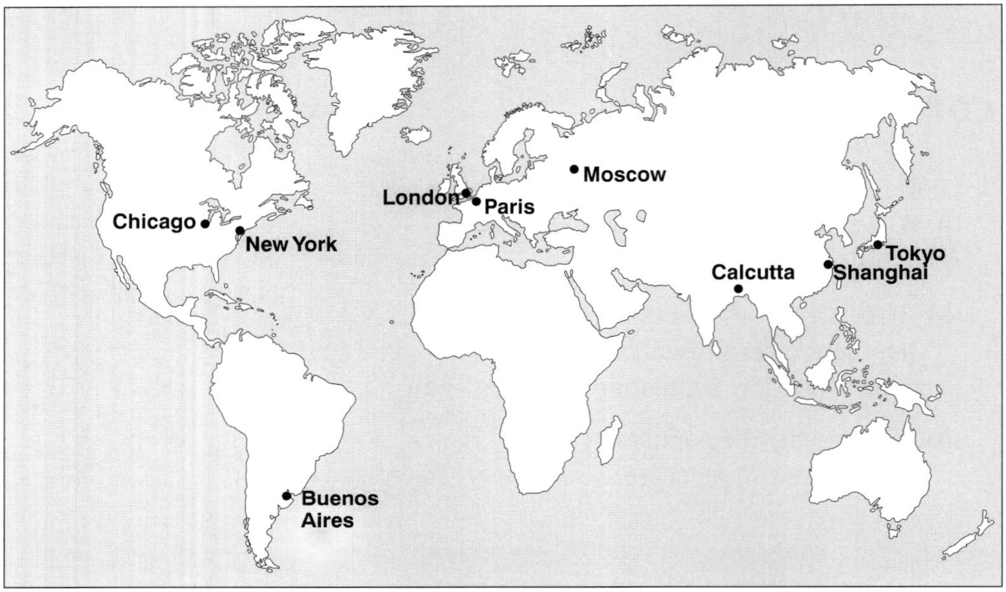

The world's largest cities in 1995

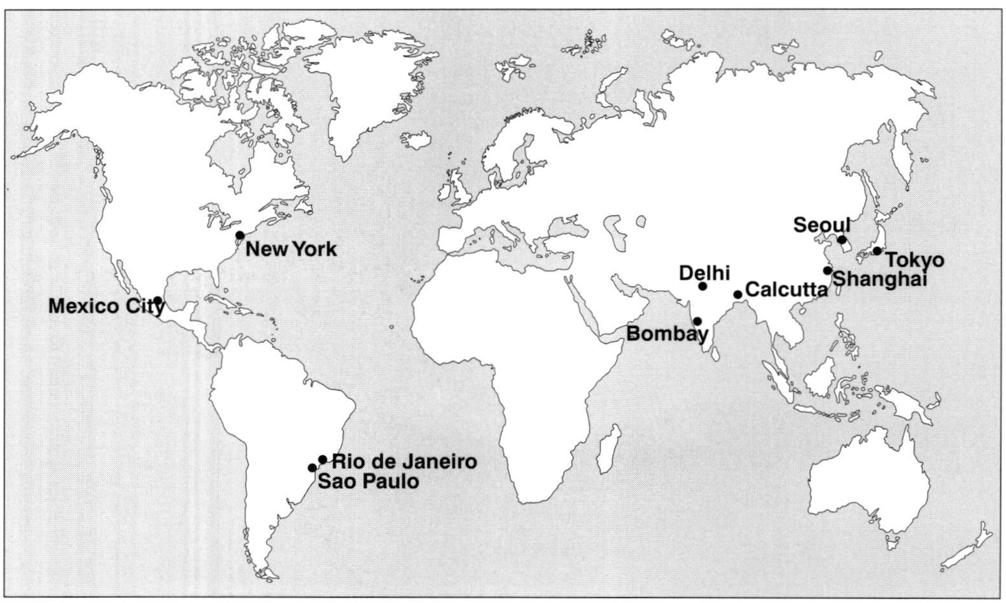

EXTENSION TASKS

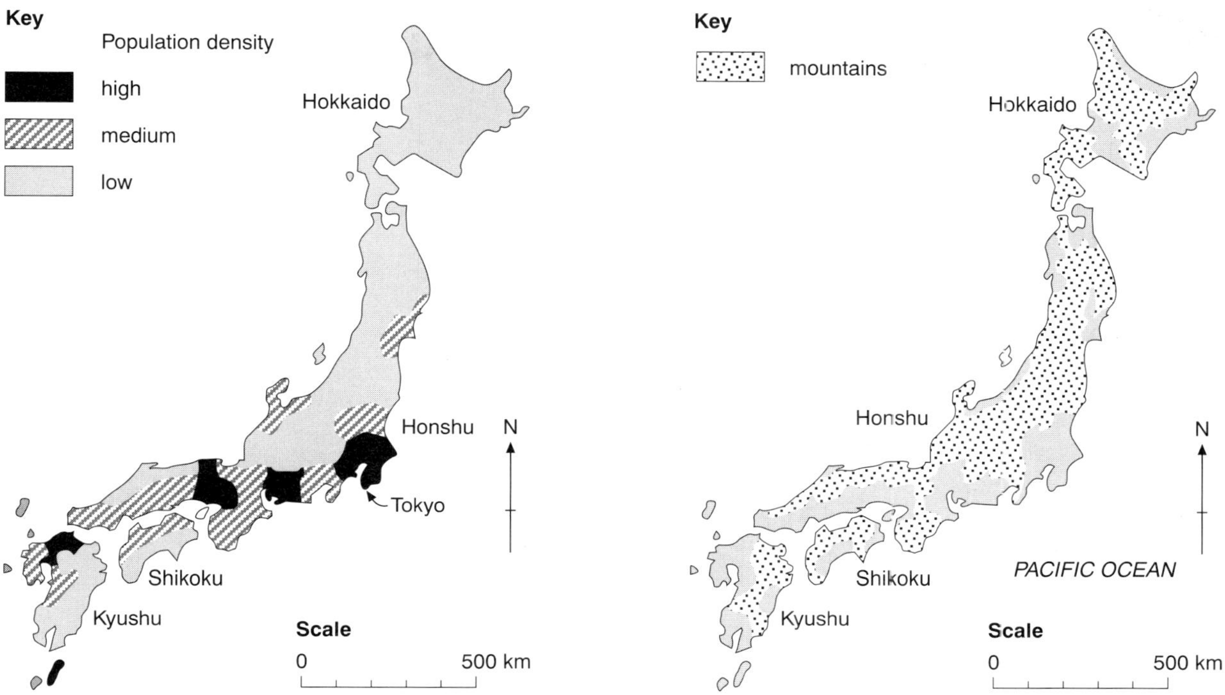

FIGURE 12.3A Information about Japan

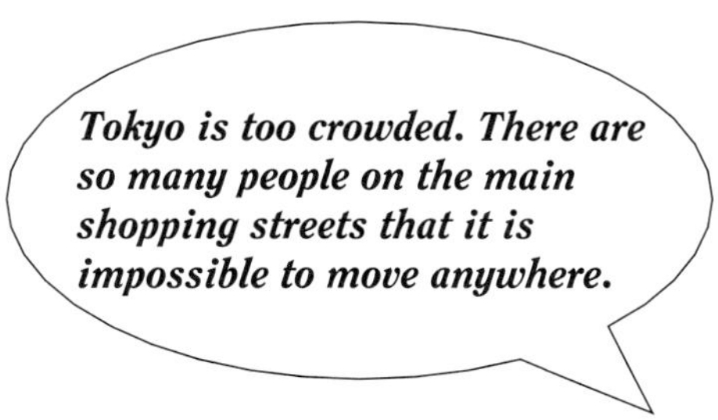

FIGURE 12.3B One person's view of the density of population in central Tokyo

3 Look at Figures 12.3A and 12.3B.

(a) Describe the distribution of Japan's population. (3)

(b) Explain the distribution of Japan's population. (3)

(c) Figure 12.3B shows one person's view about the density of population in Tokyo. Explain why this view is an exaggeration. (3)

(d) What problems result from overcrowding in cities such as Tokyo? List three different problems. (3)

(12)

4 Population density can be explained by economic, political and environmental factors. Give an example of each of these factors and explain how it influences population density. (6)

(6)

TOTAL NUMBER OF MARKS **36**

13 Characteristics of populations

Key Idea **Populations have measurable social and economic characteristics.**

CORE QUESTIONS

1 Look at Figure 13.1 which shows the growth of population in developing countries and developed countries.

(a) Describe what is happening to population growth in developing countries. (2)

(b) Describe what is happening to population growth in developed countries. (2)

(c) Give reasons for the differences between the population growth in developing countries and the population growth in developed countries. (2)

(6)

2 Figure 13.2 shows population growth rates for five countries.

(a) Identify two countries which are developing countries and two countries which are developed countries. (4)

(b) Why is population growth a good indicator of development? (2)

(6)

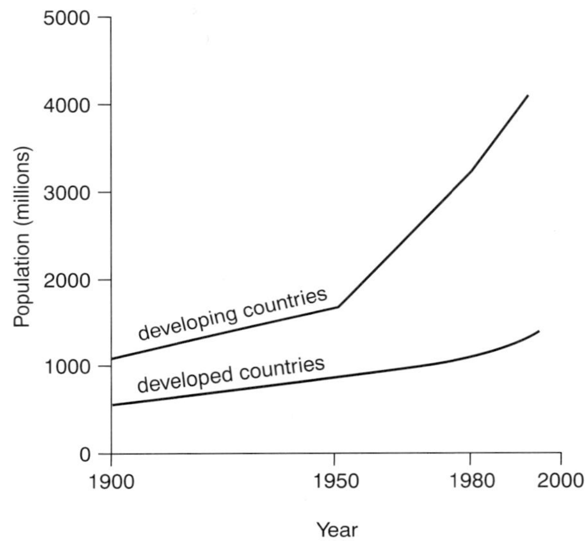

FIGURE 13.1 The growth of population in developing countries and developed countries

Country	Percentage increase per year
Ivory Coast	3.5
Belgium	0.2
Peru	2.0
Jamaica	1.8
Australia	0.8

FIGURE 13.2 Population growth rates for five countries

EXTENSION TASKS

3 Study Figure 13.3 which shows indicators of development for five countries.

(a) Choose two indicators of development from the table. For your choice of indicators, explain the differences between the figures for developed countries and the figures for developing countries. (4)

(b) Apart from the indicators shown in the table, what other indicators can be used to show a country's level of development? List two different indicators. (2)

(6)

Indicators of development	Country A	B	C	D	E
children at secondary school (%)	99	98	78	38	26
number of people per doctor	850	960	1550	4120	6500
life expectancy (years)	75	70	62	55	51
number of cars per 1000 people	470	340	180	32	2
people in agriculture (%)	8	6	35	86	92
population growth (% increase/year)	0.1	0.3	1.9	3.6	3.8

FIGURE 13.3 Indicators of development for five countries

4 Figure 13.4 shows population pyramids for two countries.

(a) Which population pyramid (**A** or **B**) shows a developed country? (1)

(b) What can be done to reduce birth rates in developing countries? State two possible actions. (2)

(c) What can be done to increase life expectancy in developing countries? State two possible actions. (2)

(d) Why are there more men than women in the 15–45 year age group in population pyramid **A**? Give one possible reason. (1)

(6)

FIGURE 13.4 Population pyramids for two countries

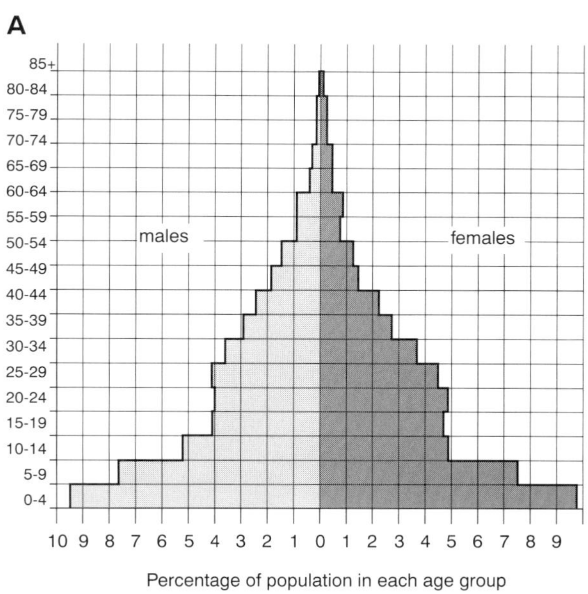

5 Look at Figure 13.5 which shows some of the problems facing census-takers in Afghanistan.

(a) Why is it difficult to take a census in Afghanistan?
Give three reasons. (3)

(b) Why, in spite of the problems, is census information important to Afghanistan? (3)

(6)

TOTAL NUMBER OF MARKS **30**

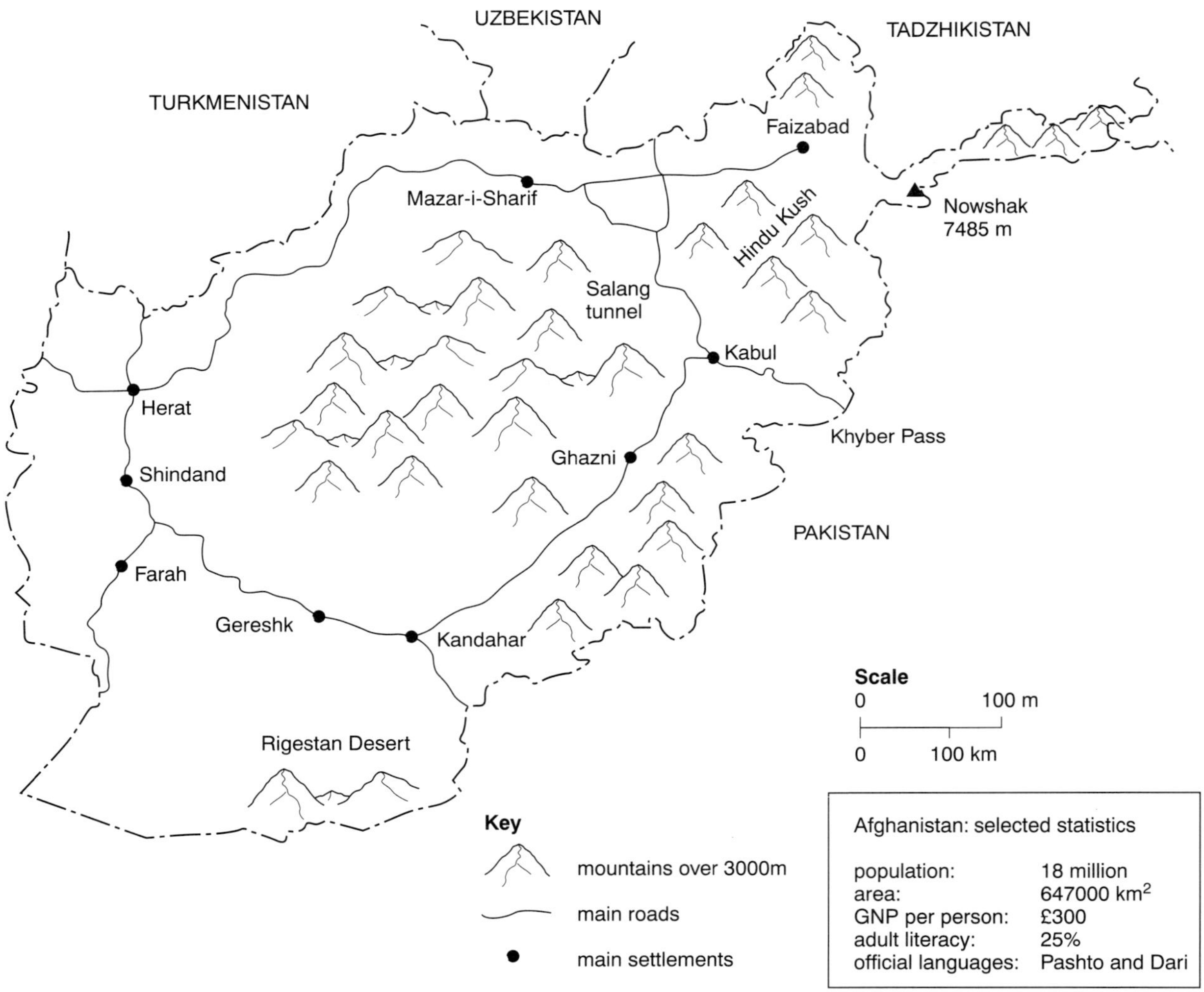

FIGURE 13.5 Problems facing census-takers in Afghanistan

14
Population change

Key Idea In any area, the size and structure of the population are subject to change.

CORE QUESTIONS

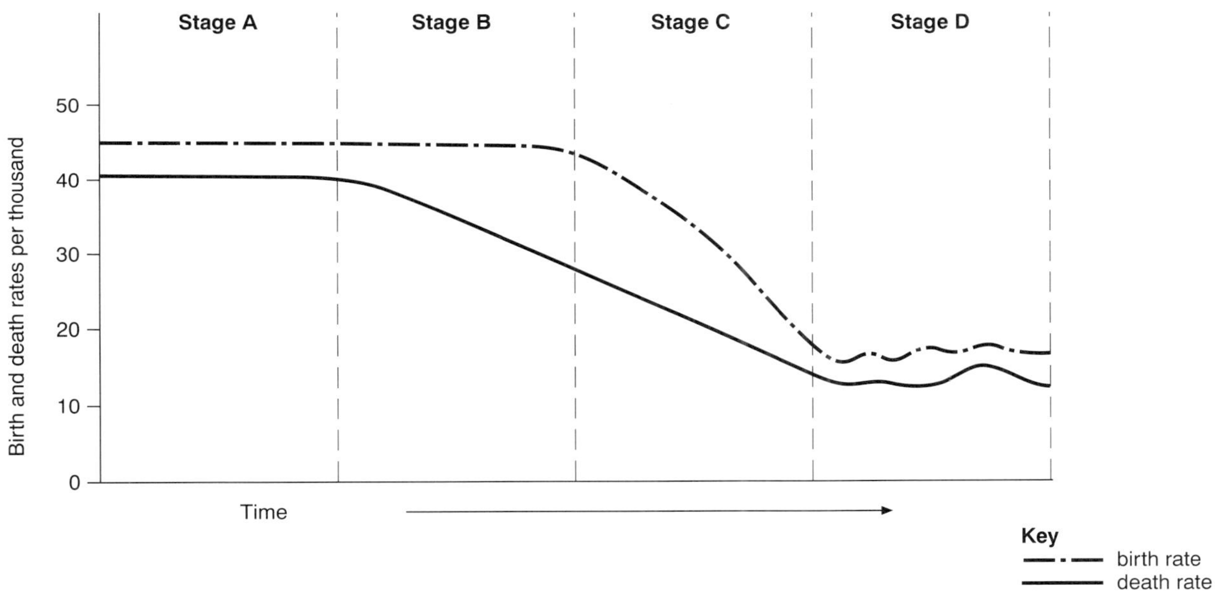

FIGURE 14.1 A model of how population changes through time

1 Figure 14.1 shows a model of how population changes through time.

(a) State which stage has:
 i. a high birth rate and a declining death rate
 ii. a declining birth rate and a declining death rate
 iii. a low birth rate and a low death rate (3)

(b) Name the stage when:
 i. the population is growing slowly
 ii. the population is growing quickly. (2)

(c) State how you can tell when the population is growing slowly or quickly. (1)

(6)

Floods have damaged houses and land in the home area.

Higher wages are available in other areas.

Better schools and universities are available in other areas.

Bad weather has resulted in a poor harvest in the home area.

Family members don't want their relatives to leave the home area.

There is a wider range of jobs available in other areas.

There is the chance of a better social life in other areas.

People in the home area don't have money for transport.

People in the home area have friends and relatives living in other areas.

FIGURE 14.2 Reasons why people migrate

2 Look at Figure 14.2 which shows some of the reasons why people migrate and the obstacles they face.

(a) List two 'push' factors which help to explain why people leave their home area. (2)

(b) List two 'pull' factors which help to attract people to another area. (2)

(c) List two obstacles facing people who want to migrate. (2)

(6)

3 Study Figure 14.3 which shows the birth and death rates for five countries.

(a) Name two countries where the population is expanding. (2)

(b) Name two countries where the population is declining. (2)

(c) Outline the problems which a declining population might create for a country. (2)

(6)

Country	Birth rate per 1000 people	Death rate per 1000 people
A	23	7
B	51	20
C	13	14
D	30	5
E	17	19

FIGURE 14.3 Birth and death rates for five countries

EXTENSION TASKS

4 Figure 14.4 shows how a population changes.

(a) State the meaning of the term 'natural increase'. (2)

(b) Copy Figure 14.4 and then add the following labels to the appropriate boxes:

immigrants deaths births emigrants (4)

(6)

5 Look at Figure 14.5 which shows migration to and from cities in the Developed World and the Developing World.

(a) Describe the different patterns. (3)

(b) Give reasons for the differences. (3)

(6)

FIGURE 14.4 Population change

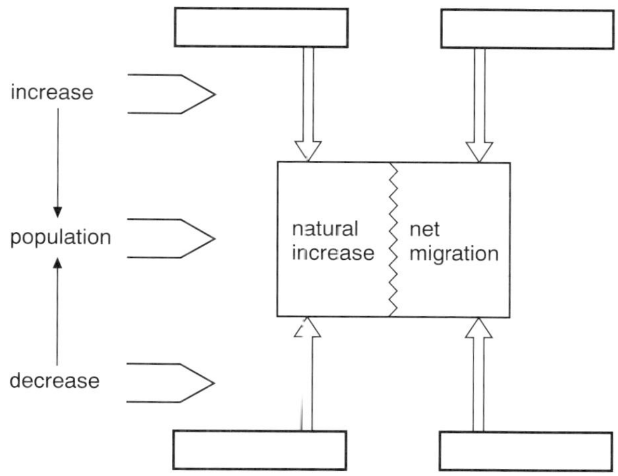

FIGURE 14.5 Migration to and from cities in the Developed World and the Developing World

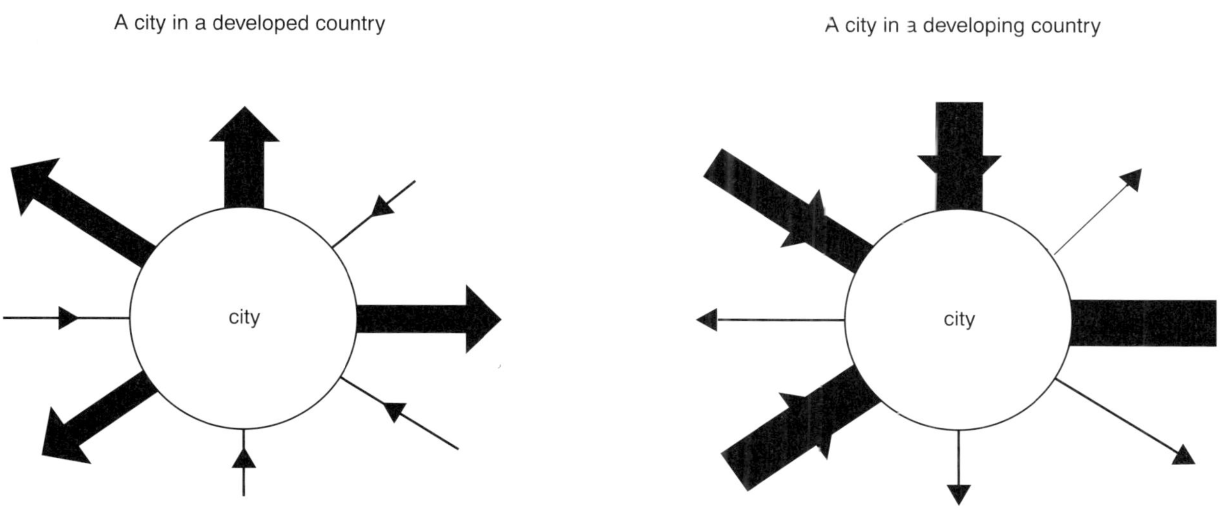

The arrowhead shows the direction of migration
The thicker the arrow the greater the number of people migrating

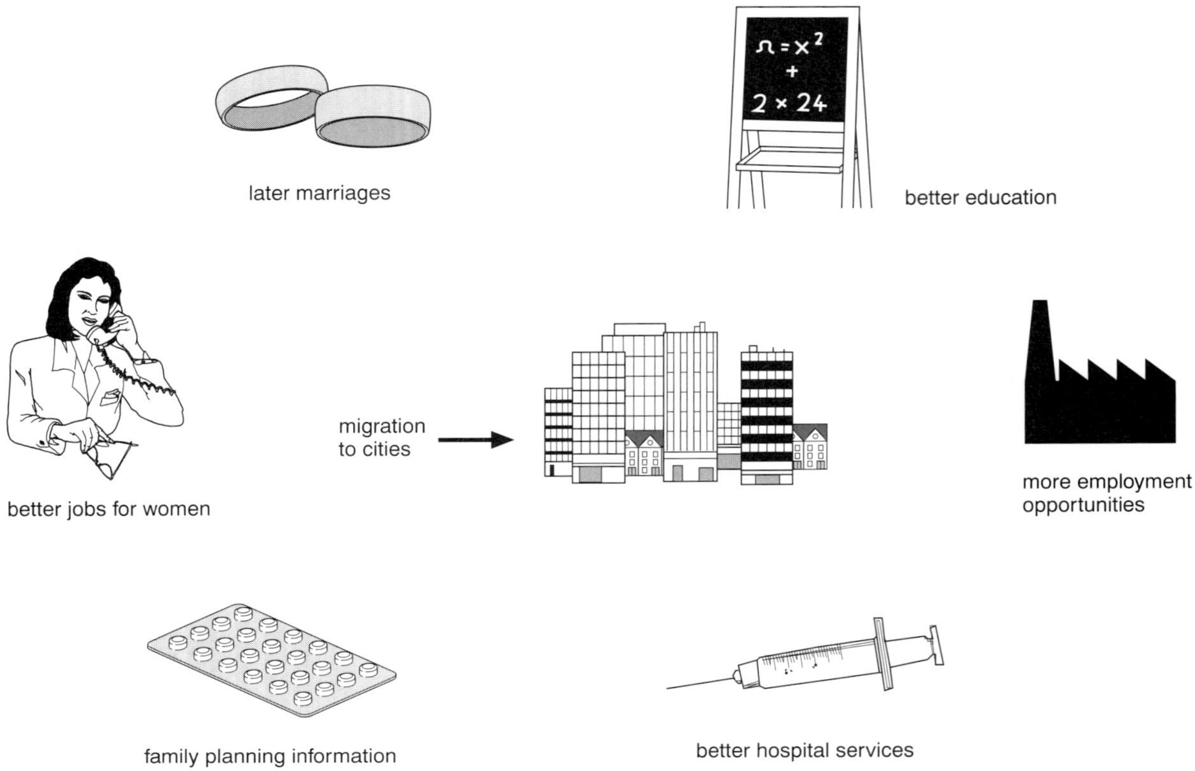

FIGURE 14.6 Factors which affect birth rates in developing countries

6 Figure 14.6 shows some of the factors which affect birth rates in developing countries. Choose three of the factors and outline how they can reduce birth rates in developing countries. (6)

(6)

TOTAL NUMBER OF MARKS **36**

15
International Relations

Key Idea

International relations are dominated by a limited number of countries acting in conjunction with others.

CORE QUESTIONS

1 Read the three newspaper headlines in Figure 15.1.

FIGURE 15.1 Three newspaper headlines

(a) State the meaning of the term 'superpower'. (1)

(b) Name two of the world's most important superpowers. (2)

(c) What helped the two countries you gave in your answer to **(b)** become superpowers? (3)

(6)

NATO OAU

NATO . . . the North Atlantic Treaty Organisation . . . including the United States of America, the United Kingdom, France and Germany . . . formed in 1949 for the defence of Europe and the North Atlantic . . . headquarters in Brussels.

CIS . . . the Commonwealth of Independent States . . . including Russia, Ukraine and Armenia . . . formed in 1991 after the breakup of the Soviet Union . . . headquarters in Minsk.

LAS . . . League of Arab States . . . including Algeria, Egypt and Syria . . . formed in 1945 to promote co-operation between Arab nations . . . headquarters in Cairo.

ASEAN . . . The Association of South East Asian Nations . . . including Indonesia, Malaysia and Singapore . . . formed in 1967 to promote economic growth in south east Asia . . . headquarters in Jakarta.

OAU . . . Organisation for African Unity . . . including Ethiopia, Sudan and Tanzania . . . formed in 1963 to promote the development of African states . . . headquarters in Addis Ababa.

FIGURE 15.2 Five international alliances

2 Figure 15.2 lists five international alliances.

(a) State the meaning of the term 'international alliance'. (1)

(b) What are the benefits of belonging to an international alliance? Give two benefits. (2)

(c) What problems may arise if two countries in different alliances disagree over a major issue? (3)

(6)

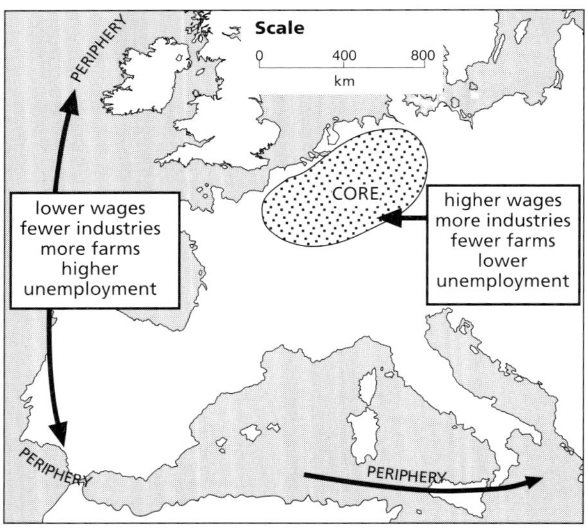

FIGURE 15.3 The European Union

EXTENSION TASKS

3 Figure 15.3 is a map showing the core and periphery of the European Union.

(a) What advantages do countries gain by being in the core of the EU? List three different advantages. (3)

(b) What can be done to help countries in the periphery of the EU? (3)

(6)

4 (a) State the meaning of the term 'flashpoint'. (2)

(b) Name two flashpoints in the world today. Explain why each is a flashpoint. (4)

(6)

TOTAL NUMBER OF MARKS **24**

16 Trade

Key Idea **Regions of the world are linked through trade.**

CORE QUESTIONS

1 Figure 16.1 shows the value of Japanese exports, 1960–95.

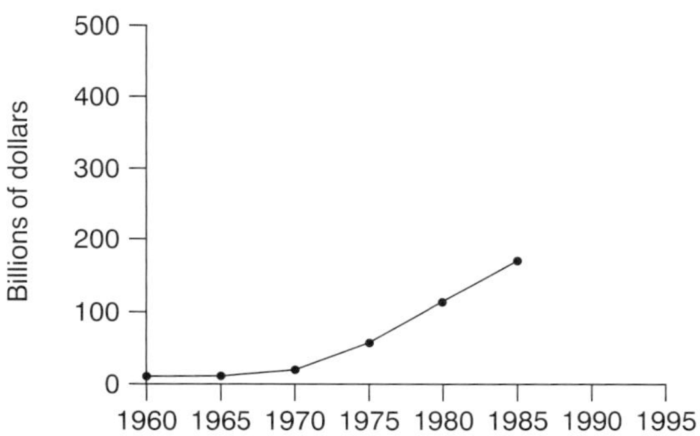

FIGURE 16.1 The value of Japanese exports, 1960–95

(a) Copy and complete the graph using the following information:

Year	Value of exports (billion US dollars)
1990	280
1995	420

(3)

(b) Describe what happened to the value of Japanese exports between:

i. 1960 and 1965

ii. 1975 and 1980. (3)

(6)

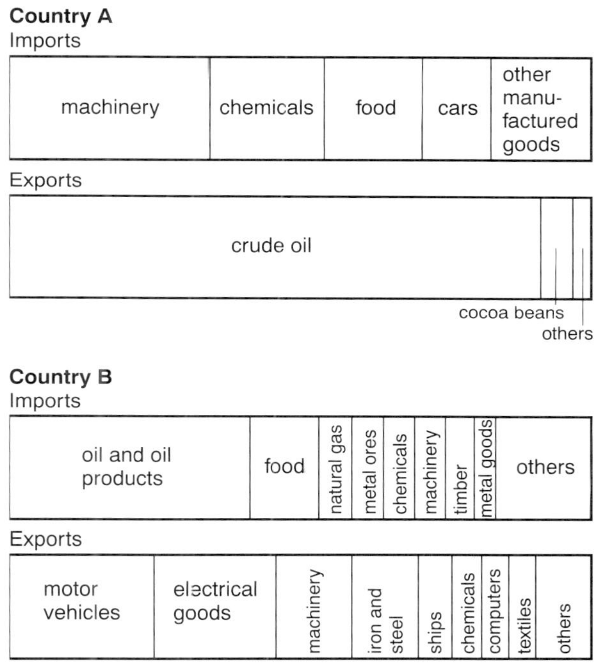

FIGURE 16.2 The trade patterns of two countries

2 Figure 16.2 shows the trade patterns of two countries.

(a) Which country (**A** or **B**) is a developed country? Give two reasons for your answer. (3)

(b) Which country (**A** or **B**) is a developing country? Give two reasons for your answer. (3)

(6)

EXTENSION TASKS

3 Look at Figure 16.3 which shows one country's balance of trade.

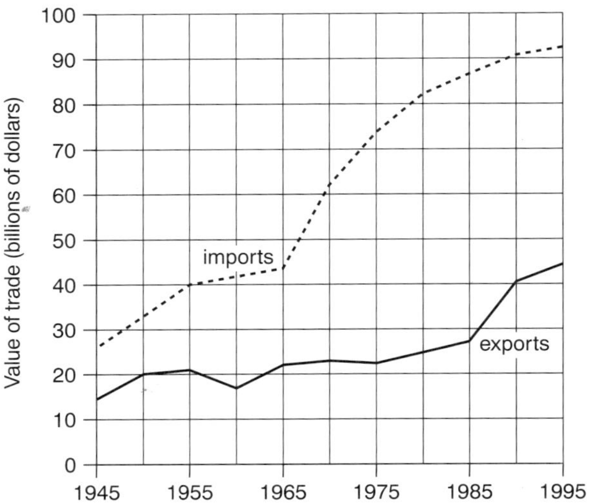

FIGURE 16.3 One country's balance of trade

(a) Does the graph show a trade deficit or a trade surplus? Give a reason for your answer. (2)

(b) Outline the problems which may result if a country develops a large:

i. trade deficit

ii. trade surplus. (4)

(6)

4 **(a)** What are the advantages of being a member of a large trading alliance such as the European Union? (3)

(b) What steps are taken to prevent large amounts of imports entering the European Union from non-member states? (3)

(6)

TOTAL NUMBER OF MARKS **24**

17
Aid

Key Idea

Schemes of self help, along with national and international aid, seek to encourage social and economic development.

CORE QUESTIONS

1 Figure 17.1 shows the average number of deaths, in a year, caused by natural disasters.

(a) After a natural disaster both short-term and long-term aid is required. Choose one of the natural disasters mentioned in Figure 17.1. Give two examples of the aid which would be required in the short term, and two examples of the aid which would be required in the long term. (4)

(b) What international organisations might help to organise aid to countries affected by natural disasters? Name two different organisations. (2)

(6)

FIGURE 17.1 The average number of deaths (per year) caused by natural disasters

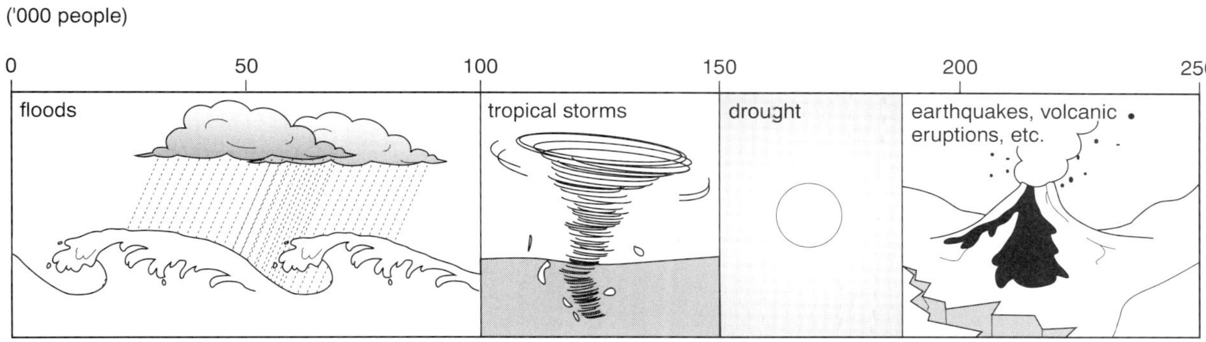

2 Look at Figure 17.2 which shows various statistics for three countries.

FIGURE 17.2 Statistics for three countries

Indicators of development	Country A	Country B	Country C
Life expectancy (years)	75	49	67
Adult literacy rate (% of population)	99	28	95
Birth rate (per 1000 people)	12	55	18

(a) Which of the three countries requires aid. Give two reasons for your choice. (3)

(b) What sort of aid would benefit this country? (3)

(6)

FIGURE 17.3 'The Divided Planet'

The rich 'North' including Canada, the USA, Europe and Japan:

- accounts for 25 per cent of the world's population
- produces 85 per cent of the world's industrial goods
- consumes 80 per cent of the world's energy
- pays an average of 4 per cent interest on its foreign debts
- has 500 million people who earn more than £15 000 a year.

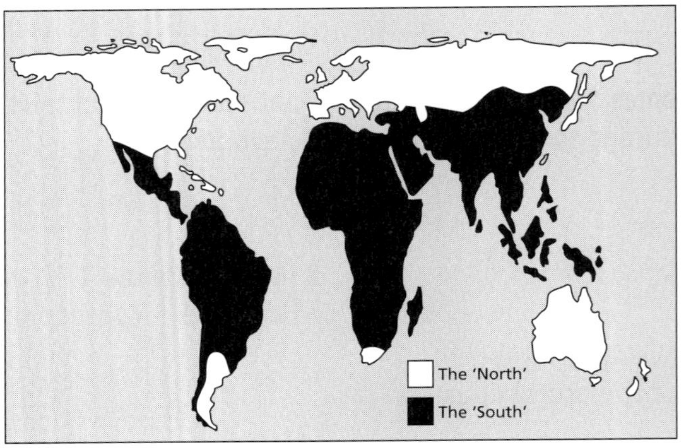

The poor 'South' including Brazil, India and most of the countries of Africa:

- accounts for 75 per cent of the world's population
- produces 15 per cent of the world's industrial goods
- consumes 20 per cent of the world's energy
- pays an average of 17 per cent interest on its foreign debts
- has three billion people who earn less than £200 a year.

3 Figure 17.3 shows 'The Divided Planet'.

(a) Explain why the world is described as 'The Divided Planet'. (3)

(b) Describe how international aid can reduce some of the differences between the 'North' and the 'South'. (3)

(6)

EXTENSION TASKS

4 Look at 17.4 which shows different types of aid.

FIGURE 17.4 Different types of aid

charity aid	**bilateral aid**	**multilateral aid**
from voluntary organisations; usually short-term aid	from one government to another government; often tied (with strings attached)	usually through United Nations' organisations such as the World Health Organisation

(a) State the meaning of the following terms:
 i. charity aid
 ii. bilateral aid
 iii. multilateral aid. (3)

(b) Bilateral aid is often tied aid. With the help of an example state what 'tied aid' means. (3)

(6)

5 Study Figure 17.5A, a photograph of a house in a shanty town, and Figure 17.5B, some views about shanty towns.

(a) State the meaning of the term 'shanty town'. (1)

(b) Outline ways in which houses in shanty towns might be 'unfit for human habitation'. (2)

(c) State three reasons for the growth of shanty towns in cities in Developing Countries. (3)

(6)

FIGURE 17.5A A house in a shanty town

FIGURE 17.5B Comments about shanty towns

Shanty towns are unfit for human habitation.

Shanty towns have become an important part of the geography of cities in developing countries.

Shanty towns enable poor people to help themselves.

Shanty towns prevent people from sleeping on the street.

Shanty towns are dangerous eyesores.

6 Read Figure 17.6 which describes the efforts being made by local people to improve conditions in a shanty town in São Paulo, Brazil.

(a) In what ways is the work of the Riverside Co-operative an example of a self-help scheme? (3)

(b) Outline the advantages of self-help schemes. (3)

(c) What can city governments do to assist self-help schemes? (3)

(d) Suggest ways in which developed countries can help to reduce poverty and disease in developing countries. (3)

(12)

TOTAL NUMBER OF MARKS **42**

FIGURE 17.6 Self-help in a shanty town

SELF HELP IN RIVERSIDE
25.3.96
Riverside, São Paulo.

Residents in São Paulo's Riverside shanty town have formed a co-operative in an attempt to improve their living conditions. A spokesperson for the Riverside Co-operative says the skills of local people will be used to improve the area's houses, roads and water supply and to build a new community centre where the co-operative will have its main office. The co-operative is also encouraging people to clear rubbish away from the houses and to help clean the nearby river which provides the area with its water supply. "At the same time we are trying to raise money to provide supplies of electricity for the town," the co-operative spokesperson said. "The residents of Riverside hope that their own efforts will encourage the city government to make Riverside a legal settlement and then connect the area's houses to the city's water and sewerage system."

GENERAL WORDS

bias a distorted or prejudiced view
conflict an argument or difference of opinion
distribution the spread throughout a country or region
drainage the removal of water from the land by, for example, rivers and drainage ditches
economic factors factors connected with money, jobs and living standards
environmental factors factors connected with the environment including the land, the climate and the vegetation
exaggeration when something is made to sound much better or much worse than it actually is
field sketch a labelled drawing of the observations which have been made, and the information collected, from field work
field work the collection of information out in the open
hierarchy a list in order of size or importance
human factors factors to do with people
hypothesis a suggestion or prediction of what might be expected to happen; when starting an investigation a geographer often produces a hypothesis to test, for example: the main land uses which will be found at the edge of a city are housing and farming
land use the way in which the land is being used
location where something is
model a theoretical representation of some feature, such as a city, in the real world
physical factors factors to do with the land and the climate
political factors factors to do with the government
questionnaire a list of questions which have been devised to obtain information, opinions and ideas about a particular issue
relationships links
relief the shape and height of the land
sampling collecting a representative selection of measurements, for example, taking samples of soils to determine the types of soils which are available in an agricultural region
social factors factors to do with people and the communities in which they live

THE PHYSICAL ENVIRONMENT

air pressure the force exerted by air on the earth's surface
air stream a moving body of air
anemometer the instrument for measuring the speed of the wind
annual rainfall the total amount of rain a place receives in a year
anticyclone a high pressure system which brings settled weather
arête a knife-edge ridge between two corries
barometer the instrument for measuring air pressure
Beaufort scale a scale for measuring the speed of the wind
boulder clay rocks, sands and gravels deposited by melting ice
cold front the boundary in front of cold air
corrie a large hollow, created by glacial erosion, at the top of a mountain
deposition the dropping of rocks and other materials by, for example, glaciers or rivers
depression a low pressure system which brings unsettled weather
drumlin a smooth, egg-shaped hill formed beneath an ice sheet
Equatorial climate a hot and wet climate which is experienced in the Amazon Basin and other places which lie next to the Equator

erosion the wearing away of material by, for example, glaciers or water

esker a winding ridge of sand and gravel left after an ice sheet has melted

glacier a mass of ice flowing down a valley

hanging valley a smaller valley which hangs above the main U-shaped valley in a glaciated region

Hot Desert climate a hot, dry climate which is generally experienced on the western sides of continents around 30° North and South of the equator

Ice Age the long cold period when snow and ice covered most of northern Europe

isobar a line joining places with the same air pressure

lower course of river the end part of a river where the water is often moving slowly over a flood plain

meander a sharp bend in a river

Mediterranean climate a warm climate with dry summers which is experienced in southern France and other places which lie next to the Mediterranean Sea

middle course of river the middle part of a river where more water joins the river and its valley becomes wider and more open

moraine material deposited by glaciers

occluded front where a cold front overtakes a warm front

ox-bow lake a small lake which was once part of the meander loop of a river

polar continental air cold and dry air which flows from the north over the land

polar maritime air cold and wet air which flows from the north over the sea

pyramidal peak a pyramid-shaped peak formed by glacial erosion

rain gauge the instrument for measuring precipitation

range of temperature the difference between the highest monthly temperature and the lowest monthly temperature

spur a ridge of rock which juts into a valley

Stevenson screen a wooden, white box on four legs which holds weather instruments

sunshine recorder the instrument for measuring sunshine

terminal moraine the moraine dropped at the end of a glacier

thermometer the instrument for measuring temperature

tributary a smaller river which flows into a larger river

tropical continental air warm and dry air which flows from the south over the land

tropical maritime air warm and wet air which flows from the south over the sea

truncated spur a spur of land which has been cut off, or truncated, by moving ice

Tundra climate a cold and dry climate which is found in northern Canada and northern Russia

upper course of river the first part of a river where the water flows quickly down a narrow V-shaped valley

U-shaped valley a flat-bottomed, steep-sided valley which has been shaped by a glacier

warm front the boundary in front of warm air

warm sector the wedge of warm air between a warm front and a cold front

weather radar a machine which shows where rain is falling

weather satellite photographs photographs of weather systems sent back from satellites orbiting the Earth

wind vane the instrument for showing wind direction

THE HUMAN ENVIRONMENT

agribusiness the organisation of a farm as a business

arable land land which is used for growing crops

cash crops crops which are grown for sale
central business district the centre of a city which usually has large department stores, offices, a town hall and a main railway station
commuter village a village next to a city; many people travel, or commute, from the village to work in the city
derelict land disused land
fodder crops crops which are grown for animals to eat
function the main purpose of a settlement, for example as a port, market town or route centre
green belt an area of protected countryside around towns and cities
high-tech industry an industry, such as making computers, which uses advanced equipment
hydro-electric power electricity produced by the force of falling water
industrial crops crops which are grown for use in industry
industrial estate an area of modern factories
infrastructure the framework of roads, railways, power and water supplies
market garden a small farm which produces soft fruits, flowers and vegetables
market town a town, surrounded by good farmland, which provides services for farmers
national park a protected area of countryside
new industrial landscape estates of modern factories with clean air and much greenery
new town a planned town, such as East Kilbride, which offers new housing and jobs
oil refinery a large plant where crude oil is refined into petrol and other oil-based products
old industrial landscape areas of factories and houses with little greenery and much air pollution
pastoral land land which is left as grass for animals to eat
primary industry activities such as farming, fishing and mining which involve taking resources from the land or sea
residential area housing area
route centre a place where a number of different roads and railways meet
rural areas countryside areas
secondary industry an activity, such as steelmaking or shipbuilding, which involves making or manufacturing goods from raw materials
site the land on which a settlement has been built
situation the position of a settlement in relation to other places
sphere of influence the area which is served by a service or settlement
suburb a residential area on the outskirts of a town or city
tertiary industry an activity, such as serving in a shop or driving a bus, which involves providing a service
urban areas towns and cities
urban renewal improving old and rundown parts of towns and cities

INTERNATIONAL ISSUES

aid help
acid rain rain containing pollutants which result from the burning of fossil fuels in power stations, factories and cars
alliance an agreement or union involving different countries
balance of trade the balance between a country's imports and exports
birth rate the number of births per 1000 people
census a count of the number of people living in a country
core centre
death rate the number of deaths per 1000 people
desertification the process of land becoming a desert

developed countries countries which have high living standards
developing countries countries which have low living standards
European Union an alliance of countries in Europe
exports goods which are sold to other countries
imports goods which are bought from other countries
indicators of development statistics which help to indicate a country's standard of living
international aid aid sent from one country to another country
life expectancy the average number of years a newborn baby can expect to live
literacy the ability to read and write
migration the movement of people from one place to another
natural increase the birth rate minus the death rate (in other words, the increase in population)
negative areas empty areas where the land is difficult for settlement
periphery edge
pollution smoke, dust, noise and anything else which spoils the environment
population the number of people in a city, country or region
population change the increase or decrease in population
population density the number of people per square kilometre of land
population distribution the way in which population is spread throughout a country or region
population explosion a large and rapid population increase
population pyramid a bar graph which shows the age and sex composition of a population
positive areas crowded areas where the land and climate is suitable for settlement
pull factors reasons why people are attracted to an area
push factors reasons why people leave an area
rainforest the hardwood trees found in areas with an Equatorial Climate
self-help scheme a scheme which uses local people, and their skills, to improve conditions in an area
shanty town an area of makeshift houses which has been built on waste ground usually at the edge of cities in developing countries
superpower a powerful country which has a strong economy and a powerful army
tariff a tax which is put on goods entering a country
tied aid aid with conditions attached
trade buying and selling
trade deficit when the value of imports exceeds the value of exports
trade gap the difference between what a country exports and what it imports
trade surplus when the value of exports exceeds the value of imports
voluntary aid aid which is given without conditions